# Wise Up to Teens

## INSIGHTS INTO MARKETING AND
## ADVERTISING TO TEENAGERS

# Wise Up to Teens

**INSIGHTS INTO MARKETING AND ADVERTISING TO TEENAGERS**

by Peter Zollo

New Strategist Publications, Inc.
Ithaca, New York

New Strategist Publications, Inc.
P.O. Box 242, Ithaca, New York 14851
607 / 273-0913

ISBN 0-9628092-9-2
Library of Congress Catalog Card Number 95-070365

Printed in the United States of America

*To Debbie and our future teens—Ben, Nini, and Jimmy.*

# Acknowlegements

This book is truly owing to the efforts and support of many, who have my deepest appreciation and deserve recognition here.

First, it's only because my father relentlessly advocated the need for me to write this book that I actually labored through it. The only book I more look forward to seeing published than this is the first Burt Zollo novel. I thank my dad, too, for his always available and heeded advice during the editing of this book. Finally, I thank him for my career.

Speaking of careers, everything worthwhile I've accomplished has been artfully (an appropriate word for her!) encouraged and totally supported by my wife Debbie. What can I say ... but I owe her everything.

As pleased as I am to have written this book, I do regret the time it took me away from our three children, Ben, Sarah, and Jimmy. But I've been blessed with the three most understanding and giving kids in the world, who knew when not to ask me to go on a bird mission, to pick out their clothes, or play a game of one-on-one. I thank them for sharing me with the computer and the airlines.

My mom I thank too. She's always been supportive of every task I've ever undertaken. Now, I'm the third man in her life to be published.

Let me also thank my brother Paul, himself an author of music books, but more significantly a truly talented and unique writer and performer of songs. (The record label that signs him will show good taste and smart business judgment!) Since TRU's very first syndicated study, Paul has written our music analysis.

I've borrowed not only his insights for this book but also some of his words.

Next, I thank Paul and Ann Krouse, without whom there simply would be no TRU. Paul's interest, concern, and valued friendship assured my eventual ownership of the company.

If everyone has a mentor in his chosen career, mine certainly would be the late Dr. Burleigh Gardner, the president of Social Research Inc. and a member of the Attitude Research Hall of Fame. Burleigh's vision set the tone for TRU, and his brilliance inspired me to pursue a career in marketing research. I treasure the time I spent with him.

Perhaps most important, I thank my staff. I'm fortunate to be surrounded by so many talented, dedicated, and energetic colleagues. First, let me thank Marla Grossberg, who enthusiastically directs our syndicated study, which serves as the basis for much of this book. Marla drafted the "Teens, Products, and Brands" chapter and has been highly involved in the development of several of the innovative measures discussed in this book.

Many thanks to Christeen (notice the appropriately revised spelling) Efken, TRU's vice president and superb director of custom research. Chris has helped me develop as a researcher and, for that, I am grateful.

I also want to thank two members of our more junior staff. First, Jason Frankena, an analyst, was involved in this book at its very beginning. I appreciate the time and energy he devoted to helping me.

And, I thank Jill Klein, our office manager, jill-of-all-trades, and an accomplished Butt-head imitator, for her help in the proofing and word processing of this book.

Let me express particular gratitude to two former TRU staffers and trusted friends. First, thanks to Jackie Orenstein, without whom I doubt I would have taken the company to its next level. Second, John Baker, currently at The Richards Group, has kept me laughing and appreciative through the years. John developed the Teen Buying Control index, which continues to be featured in our syndicated study.

Let me also acknowledge Dr. Abel Jeuland of the University of Chicago and Dr. Tamara Block of Northwestern University for their contributions to TRU's Teen/Types segmentation system, which is discussed in this book. Abel directed the statistical analysis; Tamara drafted the original descriptive analysis.

Not only have I been surrounded by quality staff, I've been equally fortunate to work with so many outstanding clients. I have benefited greatly from their experiences, approaches, and insights. As someone who travels from market to market with many of his clients, I know that the quality of individuals I've been associated with has made my life more pleasurable than I ever imagined. Special thanks to: Julio Abreu, Dorothy Ackerman, Linda Anderson, Dr. Bob Bailey, Daryl Bressler, Cindy Butler, Don Coyner, John D'Acierno, Lynda Firey-Oldroyd, Meryl Freeman, Candace Fryburger, Al Gillio, Linda Ury Greenberg, Dean Goldberg, Karen Gutierrez, Karen Haring, Angela Janklow Harrington, Lisa Hillenbrand, Rick Houghton-Larsen, Roy Kempa, Katie Kemper, Gail Keough-Dwyer, John Klingel, Jennifer Levy, Mary Jane Luck, Don McGlathery, Gwen Moran, Phyllis Porter, Tina Ruddy, Sandra Ryder, Howard Schimmel, David Spangler, Molly Stewart, and Bob Wigdor.

I'll be forever grateful to Ben Kartman for teaching me how to write, edit, and age.

Thanks, too, to my publisher, Penelope Wickham, and my editor, Cheryl Russell, for their collective enthusiasm, patience, and flexibility in working with me.

Special thanks to my friend Steven Elrod, whose counsel I regularly seek, whose opinions I greatly value, and whose support TRU and I always have.

Finally, I want to note my gratitude to my father-in-law, Mitchell Fisch. I'll never forget all the business war stories he shared with me from which I learned much, or the interest he came to take in me.

But, of course, there are always many more individuals to thank, especially those whose professional association or friendship lent support and encouragement to TRU over the years: Jon Agay, Arlyn Brenner, Bill Ewing, Jerry Ferdinand, Bruce Frank, Richard Greenswag, Steve Gomberg, Susan Herr, Stuart Himmelfarb, Eric Huvendick, Scott Kohn, Sid Levy, Jerry Medansky, Gina Perenchio, Barbara Roberts, Al Robles, Jayne Rose, Richard Rosenberg, Gary Rudman, Jay Silverman, Gale Strenger, Candi Schwartz, and Gary Zemtseff.

# Table of Contents

# Tables

## 4. Teen Activities and Interests

## 5. Teen Trends and Social Hierarchy

## 6. Teens and Music

## 7. Choosing the Right Celebrity

## 8. Teen Values

# Introduction

Our company, Teenage Research Unlimited, is fortunate to specialize in what's arguably the most fascinating, challenging, and quickly changing age segment: teenagers.

The challenge for anyone who studies teenagers is that each of us was once a teen ourselves. Because of this experience, we carry with us certain expectations, beliefs, perceptions (and misperceptions) rooted in our memory. Unlike studying ethnic groups of which you are not a member, we've all been teenagers. This makes it inherently more difficult to view teenagers as a market segment in an objective, unbiased manner.

We used to advise our clients to forget everything they remembered about their teen years and start with a clean slate. These days, we guide our clients in employing "selective" memory. We ask them to focus on experiences—and (most important) the feelings associated with experiences—that relate to the process of growing up. It is the feelings associated with the tumultuous developmental transition from adolescence to adulthood that remain the same from generation to generation. These are the life stage truths and motivations that are fundamental and timeless.

In contrast to these timeless motivations and emotions of teenage life, the external trappings—fashion, music, social concerns, lifestyle choices, and related behaviors and attitudes—change with each teenage cohort. This book examines both areas: teenage as a life stage and teenagers as a cohort.

This book is based upon my nearly 15 years of experience as a researcher and marketing consultant with Teenage Research Unlimited (TRU), which is located in Northbrook, Illinois. Most of the data included in these pages come from TRU's syndicated study of teenagers, titled the *Teenage Marketing & Lifestyle Study*. This is the largest and most frequently published study of its type. It is based on the responses of a nationally representative sample of more than 2,000 12-to-19-year-olds; its results are released every six months. This large sample allows the data to be analyzed in many different ways, including by age, gender, ethnicity, region, brand, product, activity, and attitude. TRU has been conducting this semiannual study for more than 12 years, giving us a considerable amount of historical data with which we can show where teens are headed across a great variety of areas and issues.

Many of the insights in this book come from my experience as a research moderator. Over the years, I've moderated focus groups, mini-groups, triads, buddy pairs, and one-on-ones in almost every configuration and on almost every subject imaginable—from cars to condoms, sneakers to soda, peer pressure to partying. Fortunately (and by design), these quantitative and qualitative experiences overlap. Therefore, this book provides not only data but also the insights behind the numbers.

Finally, it's imperative to recognize that trying to understand teens is a continuing process. If I had to choose a single word to describe teens, it would be "change." Teens themselves are personally evolving as human beings emotionally, intellectually, and physically. And each generation of teens has its own set of characteristics, many of which are the result of the events and the environment of that cohort's teen years.

So, teens are at times a volatile and fickle audience. If anything, it is this constant change that is their most consistent characteristic. It is also their most challenging and endearing quality.

Marketers, too, must be ready for change to stay attuned to teenagers. At TRU, we're constantly examining and changing not only what we say to teens, but how and where we observe them, talk to them, and listen to them.

The moral is, if you're serious about marketing to teens, you need to be in it for the long run. Taking an occasional "snapshot" view can dangerously mislead you. Only by committing yourself to an ongoing program of talking to, listening to, and systematically monitoring this age group can you hope to profit from the teen market.

*Chapter One*

*Why Teens Are Important Consumers*

Coca-Cola, Mc Donald's, Dr. Pepper/7-Up, Wendy's, Revlon, Jordache, Converse, TDK, Columbia Pictures. Although this sounds like a veritable *Who's Who* of teen marketers, when I approached each of these companies about marketing to teens when TRU began in 1982, teenagers were not a primary target.

Most of these companies have wised up to teens since then. In fact, Coca-Cola has to be on anyone's short list of today's most effective teen marketers.

What convinced most of these companies, and many others, to change their strategy? For some, it was a recognition that their business could profit from teens today. For others, it was a long-term decision to develop a relationship with teens now for future payoff. Over the past ten years, many marketers have come to the same conclusion: teens are a consumer segment too powerful and a marketing opportunity too profitable to ignore.

There are two keys to success in this market: first, acknowledge the importance of teenage consumers; and second, recognize their uniqueness. Advertising and marketing that work with adults often will not work with teens. And certainly, advertising and marketing that are geared to children are inappropriate for teens. Teenagers like ownership. They demand it. They want media and products they can call their own. This characteristic, which is uniquely teen, dictates the strategies and tactics needed to communicate with teens. But there's a fine line between what works and what doesn't in marketing to teens. If teens regard marketing messages as blatantly teenlike or trying too hard to be cool, they can quickly reject not only the message but also the messenger.

This scenario strikes fear in the hearts of some of the bravest marketers. It is a major reason why many companies shy away from the teen market. Clearly, teens are a high-risk proposition.

But they're also high reward. If you can reach and communicate with them effectively, the payoff will be worth the effort.

Over the past few years, two misconceptions about marketing to teens have finally been erased, and rightfully so: one, teens are too elusive to reach (as a target they move too fast to hit with any precision); and two, they're simply too fickle. As media vehicles for youth proliferated in the 1980s and 1990s, from MTV to Channel One, teens became easier to reach than ever before. As companies realize that teens can be a viable target, they are systematically working to understand teens so they can profit from this market, creating advertising, promotions, and new products specifically for teens.

Marketers are rethinking their teen positionings for reasons that range from demographic to sociological. There are six key reasons why teens are such an important segment, and why more companies are jumping on the teen bandwagon every day.

**1. Teens are important because of their discretionary spending power.** How much teens spend continues to be the subject of more media stories about the teen market than all others combined. Their spending is staggering—nearly $100 billion a year—astounding reporters and marketers alike. Our firm probably gets at least ten calls a week from reporters, with questions ranging from teen vegetarianism to what's hot in fashion. But probably 80 percent of the questions are what we've come to refer to as "the teen market story."

I must admit, we enjoy these interviews least of all, because the reporters want to know only the basics: how much money teens spend and earn. We've recited these figures more times than any of us care to admit, but there's no escaping just how compelling they are. Combined with population trends, the

# Teen Spending

*Although boys have more of their own money to spend, girls spend more of their family's money.*

**(average weekly spending of teenagers, own money spent, and family money spent, by gender and age, 1994)**

|  | total money | own money | family money |
|---|---|---|---|
| **Total** | **$66** | **$39** | **$27** |
| Boys | 68 | 44 | 24 |
| Girls | 65 | 34 | 31 |
| Aged 12 to 15 | 48 | 22 | 26 |
| Aged 16 to 17 | 68 | 41 | 27 |
| Aged 18 to 19 | 102 | 74 | 28 |

Source: TRU *Teenage Marketing & Lifestyle Study*

numbers have convinced quite a few marketers to get serious about teens.

In the 1980s, we called teens SKIPPIES (School Kids with Income and Purchasing Power) to help open marketers' eyes to the vast potential teens represent. Back then, we at TRU spent as much time trying to convince companies of the viability of the teen market as helping them understand teens. These days, companies are coming out of the woodwork to market to teens, saving researchers from having to invent any more lame acronyms and allowing us instead to concentrate on the business of researching teens. So, on with the numbers.

Teens spent $63 billion of their own (earned) money in 1994, according to projections by TRU. Combined with the family money they spend, teens spend more than several states put together—an amount equivalent to half of the U.S. defense budget! Teens still spend their money on typical teen products such as music, snack foods, cosmetics, and clothes. They also spend it on some new categories, such as family groceries, computers, and even pagers. (The next chapter discusses in detail the many things teens buy.)

Teenage boys spend an average of $44 a week of their own money, while girls spend $34. Although boys have more of their own money to spend, girls spend more of their family's money. Consequently, the difference in spending between teenaged boys and girls narrows to just $3 a week.

Boys have more of their own money to spend than girls because their incomes are greater. Only part of this disparity can be explained by the fact that boys work at paying jobs about an hour a week more than girls do. So, boys either work for higher wages than girls do or they receive more money from their

# Teen Income

*Overall, teen boys have a weekly income of $76,
compared to $58 for girls.*

**(average weekly income of teenagers by gender and age, 1994)**

|  | *average weekly income* |
|---|---|
| **Total** | **$67** |
| Boys | 76 |
| Girls | 58 |
| Aged 12 to 15 | 27 |
| Aged 16 to 17 | 75 |
| Aged 18 to 19 | 144 |

Source: TRU *Teenage Marketing & Lifestyle Study*

parents for their own spending than do girls. Overall, teen boys have a weekly income of $76 compared to $58 for girls.

Teens get their money from a variety of sources. In fact, we like to think of teens as having a more diversified income portfolio than most adults. Because of this, their income is more stable (although not entirely protected) than that of adults.

In 1994, American teens had a combined income of $96 billion, up from $86 billion in 1993 and the first increase since 1991. Although teens think they're insulated from national economic trends, teen income rises and falls with the economy. Many parents say that if they're suffering financially, their children will be the last to feel it. But when the economy dips, teen income also drops, because much of it comes from parents. Similarly, when the economy is on the upswing, so is teen income.

The older the teen, the more likely he or she is to have a regular job. Younger teens are more dependent on an allowance and as-needed money given to them by their parents. Not surprisingly, older teens earn and spend much more money than do younger teens.

Not only are today's teens earning and spending significant sums of money, they are gaining experience in handling money. More than nine out of ten are involved in a financial transaction (spending or earning) every week. About two-thirds have savings accounts; almost one-third of 18- and 19-year-olds hold a credit card in their name; 17 percent of teens own stocks or bonds. Additionally, nearly 20 percent of teens have checking accounts and 9 percent have certificates of deposit. Nine percent have access to a credit card in their parents' name, and 45 percent say they would like to have a credit card in their own name.

# Where Teens Get Their Money

*Because teens get their money from a variety of sources,*
*their income is more stable than that of adults.*

**(percent of teens receiving income from source, 1994)**

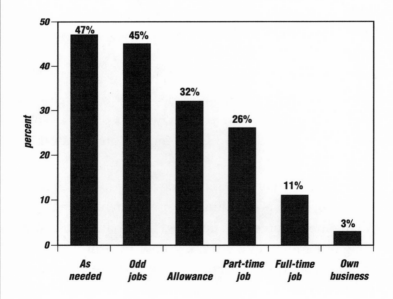

Source: TRU *Teenage Marketing & Lifestyle Study*

**2. Teens are important because they spend family money.** Because most teens live in families with two working parents or a single parent, they are assuming greater responsibility for household shopping than did teens in the past. Simply put, teens are sometimes the only family members who have time to stand in line at the grocery store.

More than half of teenage girls and more than one-third of teen boys do some food shopping each week for their family. Most just do fill-in shopping, but some are responsible for major household shopping.

When teens shop for the family, they're making brand decisions and developing buying habits and loyalties. Most teen food shoppers go to the store with a list prepared by Mom. But the list is typically generic. Instead of specifying "Hellmann's," for example, it simply says "mayonnaise." In this scenario, most teens choose the same brand they're used to seeing in their refrigerator or cupboard. But for a smaller segment of teens, a more rebellious nature emerges even in the mundane setting of a grocery store. These teens seem to say, "Mom buys Hellmann's ... hell if I'm going to!"

TRU projects that teens spent a total of $36 billion of family money in 1994. Notably, this figure does not include the family spending that is influenced by teenagers. Consequently, the total economic impact of teenagers significantly exceeds the $99 billion of their own and family money that teens spent in 1994.

**3. Teens are important because they influence their parents' spending.** Teens influence their parents' purchases in four all-too-familiar ways.

First, when teenagers (or children) accompany their parents to the store, their parents often let them add some "gimmes" to

# Teen Income Tied to Economy

*Although teens think they're insulated from national economic trends, their income rises and falls with the economy.*

**(total teen income, 1986-1994; in billions of current dollars)**

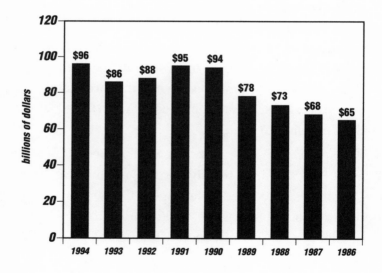

Source: TRU *Teenage Marketing & Lifestyle Study*

the cart: either the teen convinces the parent to buy something, or the teen grabs something from the shelf without much protest from Mom or Dad. (In focus groups, teens have told us about a variety of seemingly devious tactics they use to get what they want, such as sneaking items into the grocery cart or handing an item directly to the cashier, quickly bypassing their parent's eyes.)

Second, teenagers influence their parents even when they are not with them by encouraging them to buy a preferred brand. Either the teen specifically requests a brand or parents know that if they don't buy exactly what the teen wants, the purchase might go to waste.

Third, teens influence adult purchases when parents actively seek their counsel. Teens often know more about certain products than their parents do, such as computers, stereos, or the latest brand of designer jeans. Many parents consult with their in-house expert before buying these and other items.

Four, teens influence parent purchasing when they ask for gifts, since teens are rarely shy about letting their parents know what they want for their birthday or other special holiday.

**4. Teens are important because they are trendsetters.** There is probably no age group more involved with trends than teens. Not only are they trendsetters for one another, they are also trendsetters for the population at large. Blue jeans and rock music are just two examples of what can happen when teens embrace an idea. Teen influence extends beyond fashion and culture, however, affecting the nation's economy in a big way.

Younger children, being aspirational, look up to teens and often quickly adopt the latest in teen fashion. (Of course, as soon as teens see little kids sporting their look, they quickly discard it.) Adults, too, look to teens to see what's "in." As is the case with younger children, when teens see adults dressing like them, it's the kiss of death for those fashions, since teens prefer things that are uniquely their own.

A few years ago, a reporter for a leading financial newsletter called our office. Assuming it was another case of "the teen market story," I was prepared to give the reporter the latest figures on teen earning and spending. But the writer explained his innovative angle. Recognizing the enormous economic power of the teen market and teens' trendsetting ability, he asked me to predict the products or brands that would be popular in the coming year among teens, so he could advise his readers to buy the stocks of those companies! (In fact, TRU has developed the Teen Market Opportunity Index, which allows us to make these kinds of predictions. This is described in Chapter Two.)

**5. Teens are important because of the money they will spend in the future.** The most forward-thinking companies actively market adult brands to teens. If you sell acne medicine, video games, or soft drinks, marketing to teens is a mandate. But if you sell credit cards, automobiles, or newspapers, targeting teens is a less obvious and bolder move.

Camel cigarettes is an example of a brand that has been accused of developing a character (Joe Camel) that appeals to youth. Camel has vehemently denied intentionally attracting an under-age market. But other adult brands are actively developing relationships with teens, hoping this effort will pay off as teens enter adulthood. We have worked with a number of companies in building brand awareness among teens. We conducted research to assist Discover Card to develop and monitor its youth marketing programs, which include a magazine about personal finance distributed in schools, as well as college scholarships and special events. These programs create a strong, positive, and relevant relationship with young consumers. We also helped General Motors (GM) and its publishing partner, General Learning, assess the appeal of a magazine GM distributes through high school driver-education classes. In another GM project, we conducted a series of focus groups with teens and parents to gauge the appeal and enhance the concept of a program to form a parent-teen partnership in driver's education. Designed to promote safety, this type of program can build goodwill for a brand among both teens and parents. Both Discover Card and GM are betting that once teens enter the age groups in which they buy these products, they will be more likely to think of their brands because of these efforts.

TRU's Kids Research Unlimited division worked with the *Chicago Tribune* in its development of *KidNews*, a weekly newspaper within the newspaper for "tweens" (8-to-14-year-olds). It has become the prototype for children's newspaper supplements nationwide. Former *Tribune* senior editor Cokie Dishon, who developed the editorial concept and has since developed a teen supplement to *Parade*, was not only committed to developing a quality newspaper for this age group but is also a brand marketer who thinks long term. Cokie was determined to get children and young teens accustomed to reading a real newspaper. To accomplish this, she insisted that "hard news" be a major section in each issue. She also decided not to downsize the paper to fit smaller hands, believing that by familiarizing young readers with a full-sized newspaper, they would naturally graduate to the adult version once they were ready.

**6. Teens are important because there will be more of them in the years ahead.** When the founders of TRU (Paul Krouse, my father Burt Zollo, Dr. Burleigh Gardner, and I) first contemplated launching a teen-research firm in 1982, like all reasonably intel-

# Teen Population Is Expanding

*The teen population should continue to expand until the year 2010 as the children of baby boomers swell the ranks of 12-to-19-year-olds.*

**(number of 12-to-19-year-olds in millions, 1995-2010)**

|      | *number (millions)* |
|------|---------------------|
| 1995 | 29.1 |
| 2000 | 31.7 |
| 2005 | 33.9 |
| 2010 | 34.9 |

Source: U.S. Bureau of the Census

ligent marketers we checked out the demographics. Specifically, we looked at trends in the U.S. teen population. We discovered that the teen segment was projected to decline until 1992. Reflecting the fact that it's all in how you interpret the data, we figured that if we could survive the first ten years, it would be smooth sailing after that. Fortunately, we were right. Corporate America is now recognizing the opportunity presented by teens. We no longer need to sell the merits of the market, concentrating instead on helping our clients profit from it.

The teen population began to decline in 1976, after the last of the baby boomers aged out of their teen years. After 16 years of continuous decline, a turnaround occurred in 1992, as projected by demographers. In 1995, there were 29 million people aged 12 to 19 in the United States, about 1 million more than in 1994. This teen growth spurt is still in its infancy: the teen population should continue to expand until the year 2010 as the children of baby boomers swell the ranks of 12-to-19-year-olds. Because of teens' increased spending, the teen population boom creates a powerful synergy: more teens spending more money. No wonder so many marketers are now vying for teenage attention and favor.

We define the teen years as beginning at age 12, because that's the marketing world's definition of when teenage begins. We didn't always define it this way. The youngest respondents in our first syndicated studies were aged 13. But we soon discovered that marketers and the media define the teen target as aged 12 to 17 or sometimes 12 to 19. We soon changed the age range of our sample and have been tracking 12-year-olds ever since.

At its youngest end, the 12-to-19 target includes pre-pubescent children who are just entering middle school. At the oldest end are young adults in college or with full-time jobs. So it is critical to keep in mind the size and diversity of this age group. Teens also can be differentiated by gender, race, ethnicity, household income, and region. And they can be segmented by attitudes and lifestyles. Clearly, the teen market is not an easy one to target, but the rewards for doing so successfully are well worth the effort.

*Chapter Two*

*Teens, Products, and Brands*

The stereotype of today's teen is a brand-obsessed, label-driven, mall-congregating, free-spending, compulsive shopper. There is often some truth to stereotypes.

Teens love to shop. It is an experience rather than an errand, an event rather than a chore. What teens buy reflects what they think of themselves and how they wish others to perceive them. The act of buying can be one of independence or conformity, self-expression or socialization. Understanding the wants and needs behind teen buying is important for marketers of all types of consumer products.

Today's teens have the means to move brand sales in a big way. Although most adults earn more money than teens, a larger share of teen income is discretionary. Teens aren't saddled with mortgage or utility bills. They can spend their funds freely. This fact, coupled with their rising incomes, makes teens an attractive consumer segment. If you sell traditional teen products, you already know this. Marketers of adult brands are just beginning to realize it.

Teens are unique consumers. Unlike children, they have the financial resources to make big-ticket purchases such as cars, computers, or jewelry. But unlike adults, they often need the permission of a parent before they can make such a purchase. Adults play an important role in the teen buying experience, a role that needs to be recognized and addressed.

Today's teens are more brand conscious than ever before. By understanding what teens look for in a brand, and by knowing when brand choice is important, you can begin to assess your opportunities and get a better picture of what and why teens buy.

## What Makes a Brand Cool?

Years ago, we began conducting regular, exploratory focus groups with teens to uncover how they differentiate between brands. We learned that teens don't categorize products the way marketers do. A candy marketer might think its competitive set (i.e., the alternatives to its brand of candy bar) is other chocolate candy bars, for example, or even something more specific such as "enrobed" chocolate candy bars with peanuts. To teens, the competitive set might include salty snacks, cookies, ice cream, or even pizza.

We discovered that teens have a unique way of evaluating brands and products. Brand research that works with adults may not be relevant in researching teen brand preferences. This finding helped us develop several quantitative measures for assessing teen brand perceptions.

When we began to explore the process of brand evaluation among teens, we discovered that the quality of cool is of paramount importance. Teens can quickly label a brand as either cool or uncool. One of the wonderful things about qualitative research is the ability to probe as much as possible—which is exactly what we did, exploring the meaning behind the word cool. In doing so, we uncovered the factors across a variety of product categories that mark a brand as cool. By understanding what makes a brand cool, you can develop and communicate the important cues that create a cool image for your brands.

In our syndicated study we ask: "Thinking about brands of products, what makes a brand a cool brand?" By far, the one attribute teens most associate with a cool brand is quality: two-thirds of teens associate quality with being cool. The figures for girls (69 percent) and 18- and 19-year olds (72 percent) are even

# What Makes a Brand a Cool Brand?

*After quality, the most common description*
*of what makes a brand cool to teens is that*
*it is "for people my age."*

**(percent of teens citing characteristic as making a brand cool, 1993)**

|  | *percent* |
|---|---|
| Quality | 66% |
| If it's for people my age | 47 |
| Advertising | 39 |
| The name of the brand | 28 |
| If cool friends or peers use it | 24 |
| If it's a new brand | 18 |
| If it's a brand that's been around a long time | 18 |
| Packaging | 18 |
| If a cool celebrity uses it | 16 |

Source: TRU *Teenage Marketing & Lifestyle Study*

higher. The fact that teens select quality as the number-one criterion of cool says much about their level of consumer sophistication.

I would be less than candid if I didn't admit that, over the years, a few of our clients have asked us to test what teens rightly call "crap." Evidently, some marketers think that if they package their products in hot teen colors, use a popular celebrity, or shoot an MTV-style commercial, teens will buy. They are mistaken. Teens appreciate and seek quality. This does not mean that quality in and of itself will sell a product, but it is the fundamental criterion of a cool brand. The brands teens consider to be the coolest—such as Nike, Guess, Levi's, Gap, and Sega—are all perceived by teens to be of high quality.

Quality means different things in different product categories. For athletic shoes, quality can mean durability or ankle support. For chewing gum, quality can mean taste or long-lasting flavor. These very different attributes have one thing in common: they separate brands within a category based on perceived product superiority—or quality.

After quality, the most common description of what makes a brand cool to teens is that it is "for people my age." Teens prefer things that are specifically for them, whether it's language, fashion, advertising, or brands.

Advertising performs strongly on this measure, cited by 39 percent of teens. The fact that so many teens name advertising as something that makes a brand cool reveals just how involved teens are with advertising and the importance it has in their lives.

Interestingly, the attributes of being a new brand and an established brand are equally important in teens' minds. Nearly one in five teens associates newness with making a brand cool,

# The Coolest Brands to Teens

*Nike's branding is particularly impressive, mentioned more than twice as frequently as the number-two brand.*

**(percent of teens citing brand as one of top three cool brands, 1994)**

|                | *percent* |
|----------------|-----------|
| Nike           | 38%       |
| Guess          | 17        |
| Levi's         | 16        |
| Gap            | 11        |
| Sega           | 10        |
| Pepsi          | 8         |
| Coca-Cola      | 8         |
| Sony           | 8         |
| Reebok         | 7         |
| Girbaud        | 5         |
| Cover Girl     | 5         |
| Adidas         | 4         |
| Fila           | 3         |
| Mustang        | 3         |
| Converse       | 3         |
| Stussy         | 3         |
| Mc Donald's    | 3         |
| Super Nintendo | 3         |
| Nintendo       | 3         |
| Chevy          | 3         |
| Tommy Hilfiger | 3         |

Source: TRU *Teenage Marketing & Lifestyle Study*

# Other Brands
# Teens Think Are Cool

*At least ten teens in TRU's syndicated study mentioned each of the following brands as being cool.*

**(brands mentioned by fewer than 3 percent of respondents, 1994)**

| | | |
|---|---|---|
| Anchor Blue | Esprit | No Fear |
| Arizona Jeans | Express | Pepe |
| Asics | Gatorade | Pioneer |
| Equipment | Genesis | Pizza Hut |
| Birkenstock | Honda | Polo |
| BMW | Jeep | Porsche |
| Bongo | K-Swiss | Puma |
| Boss | Karl Kani | Revlon |
| Bugle Boy | Keds | Sega CD |
| Burger King | Kenwood | Snapple |
| Calvin Klein | LA Gear | Sprite |
| Champion | Lee | Starter |
| Chevy Camaro | Max Factor | Taco Bell |
| Chic | Maybelline | Teva |
| Clinique | Mercedes Benz | The Limited |
| Corvette | Mortal Kombat | Timberland |
| Cross Colours | Mossimo | Toyota |
| Dickies | Mountain Dew | Vans |
| Doc Martens | NBA Jam | Wrangler |
| Dodge | Nissan | Z Cavaricci |
| Dr Pepper | | |

Source: TRU *Teenage Marketing & Lifestyle Study*

underscoring the fact that an experimental market is a fertile area for new product ideas aimed at teens.

Note that cool celebrities by themselves do not do much for a brand. Celebrities can be effective in gaining teen attention, in positioning a product to teens (or a teen segment), and in furthering a brand image. But celebrities alone will not carry your brand. More on celebrities later.

## The Coolest Brands

Companies traditionally measure the strength of their brands based on behavior: which brands consumers use and buy. These days, with the concept of brand equity widely embraced and firmly rooted in marketers' minds, researchers are now measuring what consumers think and feel about brands. But to gauge teens' attitudes toward brands, marketers need to consider teens' special perspective.

In our syndicated study we ask teens: "Thinking about brand names of clothes, food, drinks, shoes, cosmetics, videogames, cars, audio/video products, etc., which are the three *coolest* brands?" Respondents were instructed to write in more than one brand from any of these or other categories. Overall, more than 200 brands were mentioned by respondents, from Nike to Starter, Chevy to BMW, and Bud Ice to Marlboro. The five brands most frequently mentioned as the coolest were Nike (38 percent), Guess (17 percent), Levi's (16 percent), Gap (11 percent), and Sega (10 percent).

Reflecting the emotional importance to teens of wearing the right clothes and shoes, the top four responses are apparel and shoe brands. Because of this teen bias, brands within other categories are at an inherent disadvantage on this measure—but revealingly so. There's no way toothpaste could be as cool as a pair of jeans. Still, this measure distinguishes the brands that have been most successful at winning teen favor.

Advertising is a key criterion of what constitutes a cool brand to teens. It's no surprise, then, that teens' favorite television commercials correlate to their favorite brands. When we ask teens in qualitative research about their favorite ads, they typically mention ads from companies at the top of the cool brand list—Nike, Levi's, Sega, Coke, Pepsi, Reebok, and Nintendo. Nike's standing is particularly impressive, mentioned more than twice as frequently as the number-two brand.

Many of those in the second tier of coolness (after the top five) are also apparel or shoe brands, as well as top brands in soft drinks, electronics, automobiles, fast food, and cosmetics.

Note that Nintendo has two brand mentions in the list, both the corporate Nintendo and its 16-bit system, Super Nintendo. When you add these two together, Nintendo/Super Nintendo rises to the number-eight brand overall among boys. Its main competitor, Sega, registers strongly (stronger than Nintendo) just based on its corporate name, which has been the battle cry at the conclusion of its television commercials. Its 16-bit system, Genesis, however, was named by relatively few respondents.

Not only do Nintendo and Sega fare better on this measure among boys than girls, there are also notable gender differences for several top brands. Although Nike is the top brand for both girls and boys, it is particularly favored by boys. In contrast, just as many girls as boys named Reebok or Adidas.

# Brand Preferences of Teen Boys and Girls

*Although Nike is the top brand for both girls and boys, it is particularly favored by boys.*

**(brands significantly favored by one gender more than the other; percent of teens citing brand as one of top three cool brands, by gender, 1994)**

|  | *boys* | *girls* |
|---|---|---|
| Nike | 45% | 30% |
| Guess | 9 | 24 |
| Levi's | 18 | 14 |
| Gap | 5 | 17 |
| Sega | 15 | 6 |
| Coca-Cola | 10 | 6 |
| Sony | 11 | 4 |
| Cover Girl | 0 | 10 |
| Starter | 4 | 0 |
| Nintendo | 4 | 1 |
| Super Nintendo | 4 | 1 |

Source: TRU *Teenage Marketing & Lifestyle Study*

## Brand Loyalty

Today's teens are tomorrow's adults. This is why more companies than ever are reaching out to teens, hoping to develop a long-lasting relationship. But do teens return the favor—just how loyal are they as consumers?

Several times during the past several years, we've been asked to submit proposals for a research study that would determine the brand loyalty of teens. Unfortunately, the optimum design for this study is complex and expensive. (To date, no client has been willing to sponsor the research.) The study would have to be longitudinal, carefully tracking the same group of people over time starting in their early teens and continuing into adulthood. The study would monitor whether current purchases and brand perceptions influence future purchase behavior and attitudes. Although we have yet to execute this type of longitudinal study, the fact that every year or two a client requests such a proposal shows how important the issue of brand loyalty is to businesses in the teen market.

Among consumers of all ages, major brands are losing market share to private label and store brands, particularly in the grocery category. Because of this, many marketers are intensifying their efforts to develop brand relationships with young consumers. Even among brand-conscious teens, however, private-label products are making inroads.

Contributing to the erosion of brand loyalty is the fact that today's teens have far more product and brand choices available to them than ever before. Teenagers are willing to experiment with products rather than buy a brand because that's what their parents buy. Developing a positive relationship with teens is, therefore, more important for your brands than ever before.

# Brand Loyalty of Teens

*Teenagers are willing to experiment with products rather than buy a brand because that's what their parents buy.*

**(among teens who use category, percent who bought, or their parents bought for them, the same brand in the category at least two out of the last three times, 1994)**

|  | 2 or 3 times | 3 times | 2 times |
|---|---|---|---|
| Tampons* | 89% | 67% | 22% |
| Sanitary pads* | 88 | 64 | 24 |
| Contact-lens solution | 85 | 71 | 13 |
| Toothpaste | 83 | 56 | 27 |
| Bar soap | 81 | 52 | 29 |
| Camera film | 81 | 57 | 24 |
| Shampoo | 81 | 44 | 37 |
| Antiperspirant/deodorant | 80 | 52 | 27 |
| Acne medication | 77 | 53 | 24 |
| Conditioner | 77 | 41 | 35 |
| Styling gel/mousse/spritz | 71 | 47 | 24 |
| Soft drinks | 69 | 37 | 32 |
| Jeans | 63 | 29 | 34 |
| Gum | 59 | 32 | 27 |
| Potato chips | 59 | 24 | 35 |
| Tortilla chips | 59 | 28 | 31 |
| Athletic shoes | 52 | 22 | 30 |
| Fast-food restaurant | 51 | 17 | 35 |
| Nail polish | 49 | 23 | 26 |
| Candy | 38 | 17 | 22 |

*girls only

Source: TRU *Teenage Marketing & Lifestyle Study*

To determine the product categories to which teens are most loyal (i.e., the categories from which teens repeatedly purchase the same brand) we gave respondents to our *Teenage Marketing & Lifestyle Study* a list of 20 categories and asked: "Thinking about the LAST 3 TIMES you bought (or your parents bought for you) this product, how many times was it the SAME BRAND?"

With the exception of camera film, the top ten categories are all health and beauty aids. The more intimate the category, the less teens are willing to risk trying a new brand if they are satisfied with the brand they are using. Experimenting in some of these categories (i.e., feminine-care products, shampoo, acne medication, antiperspirant/deodorant) is risky. Teens fear that switching brands would jeopardize their appearance or social acceptability.

Feminine-hygiene products enjoy the greatest loyalty among teens. Girls typically are introduced to brands in this category by their mothers, and there is little experimentation after that.

In some of the other health and beauty aid categories (e.g., bar soap, toothpaste), teens use the same brand over and over in part because a parent is making the brand choice. Teens understand trade-offs. Campaigning for specific brands within these categories is less important to them than getting their way in other categories.

By the time children reach their teens, they've experimented with a tremendous number of brands that either they or a family member brought into their household or that they tried while at a friend's home. Teenagers have a sense of which brands work best for them, based on efficacy, comfort, or a variety of social or psychological needs of which they may be unaware. So, when teens feel secure with how a brand performs, particularly health and beauty aids, they regard changing brands as risky or unnecessary. This was our hypothesis about teen brand choice. Intrigued, we decided to investigate it further.

What always struck us about our brand-loyalty data (which, incidentally, have been extremely stable over the years) is that fashion categories rank relatively low in loyalty. On the surface, this finding appears to contradict our qualitative research, which shows that clothes, jeans, and shoes are the categories in which brand choice is most important to teens.

Marketers call these "badge" items, products that offer signals to the peer group about their users/wearers. Brand loyalty in badge categories typically is low because of a few key factors, such as the fluctuating popularity of "in" brands, current styles/colors, availability, and price. This is not to say that brand name is less important in these categories. In fact, we believe it's more important. Supporting this is our quantitative coolest-brands measure, which shows that fashion brands rank as four of the top five coolest brands.

So, we have an apparent contradiction: some of the categories in which teens are the most loyal behaviorally (i.e., they buy the same brand repeatedly) are those in which brand choice (i.e., caring about which brand is purchased) is relatively unimportant. Therefore, investigating the importance of brand choice, both independently and in combination with brand loyalty, is a prerequisite to more fully understanding the teen-brand relationship.

## The Importance of Brand Choice

Based on our research over the years, we believe that teens' willingness to buy or campaign for certain brands is directly related to the importance of brand choice in those categories. But

# Brand Choice Can Be Important to Teens

*Teens' willingness to buy or campaign for certain brands is directly related to the importance of brand choice in those categories.*

**(percent of teens saying, "Getting the brand of my choice is most important to me when buying (or when someone buys for me)," based on category users, 1994)**

|  | *percent* |
|---|---|
| Sanitary pads* | 56% |
| Athletic shoes | 49 |
| Jeans | 49 |
| Antiperspirant/deodorant | 44 |
| Shampoo | 40 |
| Soft drinks | 29 |
| Conditioner | 29 |
| Tampons* | 28 |
| Acne remedy | 27 |
| Fast food | 27 |
| Toothpaste | 27 |
| Mousse/gel/spritz | 26 |
| Contact-lens solution | 23 |
| Gum | 20 |
| Bar soap | 18 |
| Nail polish | 16 |
| Candy | 15 |
| Camera film | 13 |
| Potato chips | 12 |
| Tortilla chips | 8 |

*girls only

Source: TRU *Teenage Marketing & Lifestyle Study*

there are categories in which brand choice is extremely important to teens, yet because the set of cool brands within these categories is constantly changing the brands enjoy less loyalty.

To test the relationship between brand choice and brand importance, we added a brand-importance measure to our syndicated study. We presented respondents with the same 20 categories listed in the brand loyalty question and asked them to choose those that best fit the statement: "Getting the brand of my choice is most important when buying (or when someone buys for me)."

This question examines brand relationships on an attitudinal basis, while the previous measure was behavioral. The findings identify the product categories in which getting the brand of choice is most important to teens, regardless of their loyalty to any particular brand.

The rank order of this list is very different from the behavioral brand-loyalty measure. The fact that two of the top three are fashion categories supports our hypothesis about the distinction between brand loyalty versus brand choice. This distinction is also supported by our finding that teens regard brands within the fashion category as the "coolest." Athletic shoes and jeans are badge items. Their importance to teens transcends their status as consumer products. They tell others how the teen sees himself or herself and how he or she wishes to be perceived. Expensive items signal affluence, for example, and some teens want to be perceived as affluent.

Tampons and sanitary pads rank first and second, respectively, in brand loyalty. But they rank eighth and first, respectively, in brand importance. In other words, girls are likely to use the same tampon brand, yet choice of brand is less important than

# When Brand Choice
# Is Most Important

*Teens regard brands within the fashion category as the
"coolest" because their importance to teens transcends
their status as consumer products.*

**(the five categories in which brand choice is most important to teens,
percent citing category by gender, 1994)**

|  | *percent* |
|---|---|
| **Boys** | |
| Athletic shoes | 61% |
| Jeans | 56 |
| Antiperspirant/deodorant | 43 |
| Soft drinks | 34 |
| Fast-food | 32 |
| **Girls** | |
| Sanitary pads | 56 |
| Shampoo | 50 |
| Antiperspirant/deodorant | 56 |
| Jeans | 41 |
| Conditioner | 39 |

Source: TRU *Teenage Marketing & Lifestyle Study*

it is when buying sanitary pads. This difference may be explained by the fact that there are simply more pad brands than tampon brands.

Only one health and beauty aid (antiperspirant/deodorant) appears in boys' top-five list, compared to four in girls' top five. This reflects the different purchasing priorities of teen boys and girls.

## Brand Loyalty and Importance: Mapping the Findings

How do brand loyalty (buying the same brand within a given category at least two of the last three times) and brand choice (the importance of brand choice within a category) interact? To find out, we rank-ordered the 20 categories in each of these two measures and plotted them on a quadrant map.

Quadrant I shows the product categories toward which teens feel most brand loyal and for which brand choice is most important to them. Teens care about buying certain brands within these categories and repeatedly purchase the same brands.

Quadrant II shows the product categories toward which teens do not feel brand loyal but brand selective. Although teens find it important to buy specific brands within these categories, their brand of choice frequently changes.

Quadrant III shows the product categories toward which teens do not feel brand loyal nor brand selective. Teens do not purchase the same brands nor do they consider it important to purchase specific brands in these categories.

Quadrant IV shows the product categories toward which teens are brand loyal but brand indifferent. Teens repeatedly use the same brands within these categories, yet the choice of brand is not particularly important to them.

# Brand Loyalty and
# Brand Importance

*The quadrant map shows at a glance how brand loyalty
and brand importance interact for teens.*

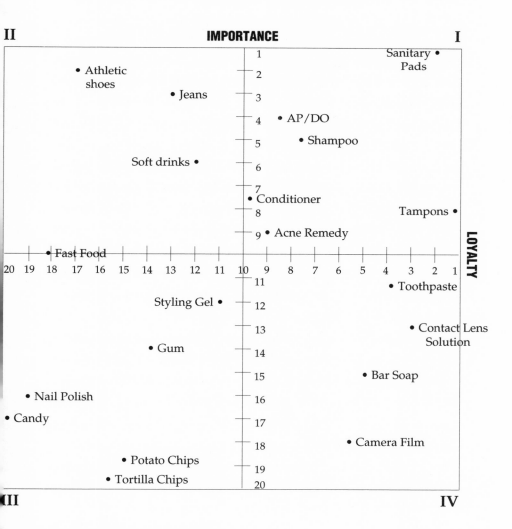

Note not only which quadrant a product category falls in but also where in the quadrant it lies. Location within a quadrant shows the degree of loyalty and the importance of brand choice relative to other categories in the quadrant. Sanitary pads and acne remedy, for example, both fall within Quadrant I, yet sanitary pads enjoy greater brand loyalty and brand importance than acne remedy.

Categories in Quadrants I and II offer marketers the greatest opportunity to develop a long-lasting relationship with teens. A brand-switching strategy would be particularly challenging for Quadrant I categories, while gaining brand loyalty is a challenge for Quadrant II categories. The big implication for marketers of Quadrant I products is to grab consumers early.

Notably, all the categories in Quadrant I are health and beauty aids (sanitary pads, tampons; antiperspirant/deodorant, shampoo, and acne remedies). These are all products for which brand switching could present a social risk. Once teens feel comfortable with a certain brand in one of these categories, they don't want to risk switching brands.

Some of the Quadrant II categories are composed of relatively large sets of acceptable brands. Teens rotate their brand of choice depending upon price, availability, and advertising. Because brand choice is important to teens when buying products in Quadrant II, marketers of these products have an opportunity to convert less-loyal category enthusiasts to loyal brand users. To exploit this opportunity, you should explore the unique attributes and perceptions of your brands and develop strategies for encouraging loyalty.

Quadrant II categories are image-oriented and heavily advertised. Several are badge items that teens use to make a statement about themselves. If a similar analysis were performed among adults, beer and automobiles would almost certainly fall into this quadrant.

Product categories plotted in Quadrant III (low loyalty and low importance) face the most difficult challenge of all. Teens neither care strongly about brand choice nor do they, even out of habit, use the same brand frequently. Four of the six products plotted in this quadrant are foods, each with many competitive brands vying for teen attention: candy, chewing gum, tortilla chips, and potato chips. Teens are less loyal to brands in these categories because there are so many interchangeable options and because low price points make it less risky to experiment. Further, purchase cycles are particularly brief for these categories. Still, it is important to remember that teens have favorite brands in snack and candy categories. Most likely, their favorite sets include several brands, suggesting that pricing and value strategies may be particularly effective in these categories.

Four product categories fall into Quadrant IV: toothpaste, contact-lens solution, bar soap, and camera film. Teens use the same brands repeatedly in these categories, but they do not regard brand as particularly important. Most likely, Mom is choosing the brand and the teen is content to use whatever brand is available. Marketers of these products need to appeal to teens directly, so that teens begin to request certain brands. Another approach would be more long-term: develop a strong relationship with young consumers, recognizing that they typically are neither the purchasers nor active requesters now but will be when they are adults.

## Teen-Specific Brands

Once your company decides to target teens, you must consider whether to develop a teen-specific product or line in addition to teen-directed advertising and promotions. Since one of the key attributes of a cool brand is that it is for "somebody my age," developing products specifically for this age group can offer some advantages. Many businesses are mining these opportunities today. In the past few years, TRU has been testing more teen-specific product concepts than ever before.

If you decide to create a teen-specific brand, an important consideration is whether to include the word "teen" or "teenage" in the product name, to communicate to teens that this is something especially for them. Why not leverage the word "teen," since we know teens want products they can call their own?

A few years ago we went to the experts, teens themselves, and asked them what words or phrases they like to be called. We found that teens prefer to be called "young" more than "teen" or "teenager."

Not surprisingly, label preference is age-related. The oldest teens almost totally reject the terms "teen" or "teenager." The youngest teens embrace these words. Twelve- to 15-year-olds have waited years to be teenagers. Now they want somebody to notice. In contrast, older teens feel the "teen" label refers to somebody much younger than themselves.

"Teen implies you're young, like you're 13!" a 16-year-old boy told us in a focus group.

"I don't like to be called a teen because the word makes you feel stupid. Teenagers have a stereotype stuck to them that all we care about is hair and makeup and getting dates and we don't have brains. That isn't true," said a 17-year-old girl.

We've also found that teens distinguish between the terms "teen" and "teenage," preferring the latter. They associate "teen" with being a young teenybopper, while "teenage" is more accepted because it is an age descriptor.

# What Teenagers Want to Be Called

*Teens prefer to be called "young" more than "teen" or "teenager."*

**(percent of teens citing label preference, 1992)**

|  | *percent* |
|---|---|
| Young men/women | 62% |
| Young adults | 59 |
| Teenagers | 43 |
| Teens | 42 |
| Students | 31 |
| Boys/girls | 14 |
| Kids | 9 |

Source: TRU *Teenage Marketing & Lifestyle Study*

Perhaps because the word "teen" is shorter and punchier than "teenage," it has been the choice of marketers. A few years ago, Mennen introduced an antiperspirant/deodorant under the name Teen Spirit, originally targeted at a teen audience. The brand found its franchise more "tween" than teen, since its buyers are younger (aged 9 to 15) than originally intended. Many older teens are turned off by the name. Commented one 17-year-old girl about the product, "The biggest turnoff is when they [advertisers] try to relate to you. Like Teen Spirit. Their ads show teens leaping in school. It's so ridiculous a name and picture that I just flip the page. You don't want to have anything to do with them when they start relating to you." Obviously this teenager is neither chronologically nor attitudinally within the Teen Spirit target market.

Teen Spirit has been successful with its younger audience, extending its brand into a hair-care line. Carter Wallace has introduced a competing Teen Image, an extension of its Arrid line.

Because teens want products for themselves, and because naming those products "teen" or "teenage" is the clearest way to communicate this, we asked teenagers how they felt about it. In our syndicated study we asked: "How likely would you be to buy products such as personal grooming items, snack foods, etcetera made specifically for people your age?" We also asked, "How likely would you be to buy products with the word 'teen' or 'teenage' in their name?"

The results supported our earlier findings. Teens prefer products made specifically for them. But they are lukewarm at best when it comes to buying brands with the words "teen" or "teenage" in their name.

# Likelihood of Buying "Teen" Products

*Teens are lukewarm at best when it comes to buying brands with the words "teen" or "teenage" in their name.*

**(attitudes of teens toward buying a product made for people their age or with the words "teen" or "teenage" in its name, 1993)**

|  | *likelihood of buying products* | |
|---|---|---|
|  | *made specifically for people your age* | *with the word "teen" or "teenage" in name* |
| **Total, more likely** | **57%** | **31%** |
| • A lot more likely | 25 | 11 |
| • Somewhat more likely | 32 | 20 |
| **Neither more nor less likely** | **35** | **45** |
| **Total, less likely** | **6** | **21** |
| • Somewhat less likely | 3 | 10 |
| • A lot less likely | 3 | 11 |

Source: TRU *Teenage Marketing & Lifestyle Study*

# Likelihood of Buying Teen Products, by Age

*The youngest teens are most enthusiastic about products with the word "teen" or "teenage" in their names.*

**(percent of teens saying they would be "a lot" or "somewhat" more likely to buy a product made for people their age or with the words "teen" or "teenage" in its name, 1993)**

|  | likelihood of buying products | |
|---|---|---|
|  | *made specifically for people your age* | *with the word "teen" or "teenage" in name* |
| Aged 12 to 15 | 65% | 43% |
| Aged 16 to 17 | 54 | 22 |
| Aged 18 to 19 | 40 | 15 |

Source: TRU *Teenage Marketing & Lifestyle Study*

Although more than one-third of teens are neutral toward buying products for people their age, only 6 percent are negative and 57 percent positive. When it comes to including "teen" or "teenage" in a brand's name, however, the neutral jumps to almost half (45 percent) of the sample, negatives rise to 21 percent, and positives drop to 31 percent.

Boys and girls are equally interested in products made specifically for their age group, but significantly more girls (37 percent) than boys (25 percent) are interested in products that incorporate the words "teen" or "teenage" in their name. Older teens are much less positive on both measures. Nevertheless, only 36 percent of the 18- and 19-year-olds and 25 percent of the 16- and 17-year-olds totally reject the idea of a "teen" named product.

As expected, those teens who are most interested in products for their age group are also more interested in products with the word "teen" or "teenage" in their names.

Teens look for and appreciate products that are made specifically for them. The challenge to marketers, however, is in the name. Calling a product "teen" or "teenage" is a turn-off to older teens, though it can increase the appeal of products targeted at "tweens" and the youngest teens. If your brand's target includes teens aged 16 or older, you should communicate that a product is for them visually or verbally without labeling a brand "teen" or "teenage."

## What Do Teens Buy?

The first question reporters typically ask us at TRU is, "Why is the teen market important?" Invariably, the second question is, "What do teens buy?" The answer is less surprising and more

# Products Purchased
# by Teen Boys

*Next to fashion, girls spend the most on personal-grooming items. Boys also care about fashion, but they spend less of their own money on it.*

**(products personally purchased by at least 25 percent of teens, percent of teens buying products in a three-month period, by gender, 1994)**

### percent of boys personally buying ...

| | | | |
|---|---|---|---|
| Fast-food/hamburger chain | 63% | Breath mints | 33% |
| Cola | 48 | Potato chips | 30 |
| Bubble gum | 47 | Thirst-quenching sports drink | 29 |
| Chocolate candy | 47 | Sports/trading cards | 29 |
| Compact disc | 43 | Fast-food/Mexican chain | 29 |
| Fast-food/pizza chain | 43 | Batteries | 28 |
| Movie ticket | 43 | Hard candy in a roll | 27 |
| Chewing gum | 41 | Ice cream | 27 |
| T-shirt | 38 | Shorts | 27 |
| Non-chocolate candy | 35 | Root beer | 26 |
| Prerecorded audio cassette | 35 | Sugarless bubble gum | 26 |
| Magazine | 34 | Gasoline | 26 |
| Cookie | 34 | Doughnuts | 26 |

Source: TRU *Teenage Marketing & Lifestyle Study*

*(continued)*

(continued from previous page)

## *percent of girls personally buying ...*

| | | | |
|---|---|---|---|
| Fast-food/hamburger chain | 53% | Sugarless chewing gum | 32% |
| Chocolate candy | 52 | Sugarless bubble gum | 32 |
| Movie ticket | 48 | Compact disc | 32 |
| Bubble gum | 47 | Ice cream | 32 |
| Chewing gum | 46 | Mascara | 31 |
| T-shirt | 44 | Prerecorded audio cassette | 31 |
| Lipstick | 42 | Eyeliner | 30 |
| Greeting card | 41 | Hair spray | 30 |
| Cola | 41 | Lip balm | 30 |
| Shorts | 39 | Lip gloss | 30 |
| Fast-food/pizza chain | 39 | Potato chips | 29 |
| Nail polish | 38 | Ballpoint pen | 28 |
| Non-chocolate candy | 37 | Camera film | 28 |
| Breath mints | 36 | Fruit juice | 27 |
| Magazine | 36 | School supplies | 27 |
| Cookie | 35 | Foundation | 27 |
| Hard candy in a roll | 33 | Moisturizer/lotion/cream | 27 |
| Casual shoes | 33 | Facial cleanser | 26 |
| Antiperspirant/deodorant | 33 | Nail polish remover | 25 |
| Book | 32 | Eye shadow | 25 |

Source: TRU *Teenage Marketing & Lifestyle Study*

predictable than most people might expect. Teens buy the same things they always have. But they are also buying products from new and emerging categories, from low-fat to high-tech. The products teens buy segment them and reveal their priorities and lifestyles.

For girls, fashion rules. Apparel is the most important product category to teen girls, consuming both the greatest proportion of their disposable income and their greatest parent-campaigning efforts. Next to fashion, girls spend the most on personal-grooming items, from mousse to mascara. With the no-makeup look becoming popular among teens, girls are using as many cosmetics as ever to achieve the minimal look.

Boys also care about fashion, but they spend less of their own money on it, preferring to convince their parents to buy clothes and shoes for them. Boys spend more than girls on food, gas, and entertainment. This includes everything from pizza, chips, candy, and burgers, to videogames, movies, concerts, sports events, and video rentals. Although boys spend less on health and beauty aids than girls do, they are a ripe market for everything from hair gel to shaving cream.

In addition to buying consumables (small-ticket items), teens are serious purchasers and proud owners of a variety of big-ticket items, from automobiles to all kinds of consumer electronics. With the exception of wristwatches and jewelry, all of teens' favorite big-ticket products provide entertainment. Teens' overriding motivation is to have fun, and they spend much of their income in this pursuit. That they are able to do so is a key difference between teens and adults, who must make sure their bills are paid before they can spend on entertainment. How often have you heard a disgruntled homeowner mutter something like, "I can't believe I just spent $800 on a hot-water

# Big-Ticket Items Owned by Teens

*With the exception of wristwatches and jewelry, all of teens' favorite big-ticket products provide entertainment.*

**(percent of teens owning, 1994)**

|  | *percent* |
|---|---|
| Wristwatch | 75% |
| Home stereo/stereo component | 72 |
| Jewelry | 65 |
| Portable radio/portable cassette player | 63 |
| TV set | 62 |
| School yearbook (hardcover) | 61 |
| Bicycle | 60 |
| Telephone | 60 |
| Sports/recreational equipment | 57 |
| Small personal stereo (with headphones) | 56 |

Source: TRU *Teenage Marketing & Lifestyle Study*

# Big-Ticket Items
# Teens Plan to Buy

*Many of the electronic products teens plan to buy are
more sophisticated versions of what they already own.*

**(percent of teens planning to buy in the next 12 months, 1994)**

|  | *percent* |
|---|---|
| Portable compact disc player | 18% |
| Home compact disc player | 16 |
| Used car | 14 |
| School yearbook (hardcover) | 14 |
| Car stereo/car stereo component | 13 |
| Computer software | 13 |
| Sports/recreational equipment | 12 |
| CD ROM drive for computer | 11 |
| Jewelry | 11 |
| Computer | 11 |

Source: TRU *Teenage Marketing & Lifestyle Study*

heater, and I get absolutely no enjoyment out of it." In contrast, if teens spend $800, they're spending it on stereos, TVs, bicycles, and other fun things.

When we ask teens which products they plan to buy in the next year, they choose consumer electronics more than any other type of product. Many of the electronic products they plan to buy are more sophisticated versions of what they already own.

To provide marketers of durable goods with a measure of how a certain product category's sales may change in the coming year, we developed the Teen Market Opportunity Index (TMO). TMO measures the increase or decrease in the percentage of teens who say they plan to purchase a certain durable good within the next year. We calculate TMOs for each big-ticket item by dividing the percentage of teens who plan to purchase an item within the next year (current data) by the percentage who said they planned to purchase the item during the previous 12 months (using data from the year earlier). An index of more than 100 suggests that a product's sales to teens are likely to grow in the coming year, while an index below 100 indicates sales may shrink.

The highest TMO index in our fall 1994 study was 121 for portable CD players. To translate, this means that 21 percent more teens in 1994 than in 1993 planned to buy a CD player within the next year. While this index does not correlate directly with sales, it indicates potential growth categories. In TRU's fall 1994 study, just under half the big-ticket categories scored at or above 100.

The TMO also identifies categories that face potential decline, either because an economic slowdown is limiting teen spending or because an item is no longer hot. If you want to portray teens in advertising, this index can tell you what's hot

# Teen Market Opportunity (TMO) Index

*Of the ten products with the highest TMO scores, five are electronic and three are directly related to computers.*

(the TMO Index is calculated by dividing the percentage of teens
who plan to purchase an item in the next 12 months by
the percentage who said they planned to buy the item
during the previous 12 months, 1994)

|  | *TMO Index* |
|---|---|
| **Potential growth categories** | |
| Portable CD player | 121 |
| Modem for computer | 120 |
| Computer software | 111 |
| Home stereo | 108 |
| Backpack | 107 |
| Camera/photo equipment | 107 |
| Musical instrument | 106 |
| Personal computer | 106 |
| Electric curling iron | 106 |

Source: TRU *Teenage Marketing & Lifestyle Study*

*(continued)*

*(continued from previous page)*

| Potential decline categories | TMO Index |
|---|---|
| TV set | 75 |
| Portable radio | 78 |
| Class ring | 80 |
| Makeup organizer case | 81 |
| Small personal stereo | 83 |
| Hand-held hairdryer | 86 |
| Electric shaver | 87 |
| Hand-held computer game | 88 |
| Home videogame | 88 |
| Telephone | 88 |
| Car stereo | 89 |
| School yearbook | 91 |
| Record club membership | 92 |
| Sports/recreation equipment | 93 |
| Braces | 93 |
| Home CD player | 94 |

Source: TRU *Teenage Marketing & Lifestyle Study*

and what's not. Of the ten products with the highest TMO scores, five are electronic and three are directly related to computers. Marketers of home electronics, particularly computers, should leverage teens' rising interest in purchasing these items.

## The Target: Teen, Parents, or Both?

Some purchases teens make for themselves; others their parents make for them. This distinction is critical and should guide you in determining whether to target teens, parents, or both.

Many companies are surprised by what teens buy for themselves and what their parents buy for them. A hair-care marketer, for example, was shocked at how involved boys are in buying or influencing the purchase of its products. Conversely, a leading acne marketer was surprised at how little involvement teens have in the actual purchase of acne remedies compared to their parents. Before you can decide how to position your products, you must understand the teen-parent dynamic.

To quantify this dynamic, a former TRU employee, John Baker (now at the Richards Groups) developed the Teen Buying Control Index (TBC). He developed the index from data we had been collecting for several years. The index is defined as the percentage of each product category that teens purchase by themselves as opposed to total purchases of the product by or for teens. The higher the TBC index, the more the teen does the purchasing and the more important the teen is in positioning and advertising.

The categories we measure fall into six general classifications: health and beauty aids, food products, audio/video products, apparel and shoes, beverages, and miscellaneous items. In each of these classifications (except miscellaneous), we calculate

# Teen Buying Control (TBC) Index: Example

*Teen girls have more purchase control over hair styling aids than they do over shampoos and conditioners.*

**(Teen Buying Control Index among girls for hair cleansers and hair styling aids; the Teen Buying Control Index is the percentage of each product category that teens personally buy themselves; health and beauty aid norm for teen girls is 44; 1994)**

| | TBC Index |
|---|---|
| **Cleansers** | |
| Hair conditioner | 30 |
| 2-in-1 shampoo | 28 |
| Regular shampoo | 26 |
| Dandruff shampoo | 25 |
| Pump/tube hair styling gel | 43 |
| Hair spray | 42 |
| **Styling Aids** | |
| Hair coloring | 56 |
| Hair spritz | 46 |
| Spray hair styling gel | 44 |
| Hair styling mousse | 43 |

Source: TRU *Teenage Marketing & Lifestyle Study*

a "norm," an average TBC for males and females. We then compare individual product categories to the norm. For example, the health and beauty aid norm for girls is 40, meaning that 40 percent of the time that a health and beauty aid is purchased for a teen girl, it is purchased directly by the girl.

TBC scores for hair styling aids are at or above the norm, while the scores for hair cleansers are below the norm. So, teen girls have more purchase control over hair styling aids than they do over shampoos and conditioners. These data suggest that girls care more about brand choice for styling products than for cleansers. Since we know that the brand of shampoo teen girls use is very important to them, these data indicate that the brand of styling aid they use is probably even more important to them. Perhaps parents are willing to buy the more basic cleansers teens prefer than the styling aids. Therefore, teen girls must buy styling aids themselves to get their brand of choice.

The difference in TBC scores for these two product categories suggests that those marketing shampoo and conditioner should consider targeting the parents of teens (since they are more likely to be the actual purchasers of these products) in addition to the teens. But those marketing hair-styling aids should target teens exclusively, since they are more likely to be the actual purchasers of these products.

By knowing how involved teens are in purchasing specific products, you can better position advertising, make the right talent decisions for this advertising, and buy the right media. The higher the TBC index, for example, the more likely that consumer promotions directed at teens, such as free samples and in-store displays, will be more effective than mass media advertising to a strong adult audience.

## Teen Influence In Purchase Decisions

We find the TBC index useful because it's a measure of the teen-parent purchase dynamic that marketers can really sink their teeth into. It quantifies how involved each party is in the purchase of specific consumer products. If a product scores low on the TBC measure, you should not automatically write it off as having no potential for a teen-targeted effort. Before doing so, you should examine the issue of purchase influence. Often, although a parent is buying it, a teen is directing the purchase.

This is a more difficult dynamic to measure. Can teens judge the influence they wield over their parents' purchases? Do parents acknowledge this influence? To find out, we talk to teens and their mothers (mothers are still much more involved in buying for their families than are fathers). Typically, we first spend a couple of minutes talking to both the teen and his or her mother, then we have a one-on-one discussion with each separately. In this way, we learn how each assesses the teen's influence and describes the parent-teen dynamic. We end the session by bringing both parties together again to discuss any perceptual gap (which there often is) and try to resolve it, if possible. This gap is quite different for consumables than it is for durable products.

Teens see themselves as being influential over the purchase and brand choice of many consumable products. But do teens think they have more influence over their parents' purchases than they actually do? In fact, just the opposite is the case. When teens think about their purchase influence, they think of how often and forcefully they ask, beg, plead, campaign for, or simply request that their parents buy them certain items. But that's not how their mothers see it. Mothers say their teenaged children are more influential than teens realize. Without the teens' urging,

# Teen Purchase Influence: Consumables

*Teens see themselves as being influential over the purchase and brand choice of many consumable products.*

**(percent of teens saying they influence their parents' purchase of selected items, 1994)**

|  | *total* | *boys* | *girls* |
|---|---|---|---|
| Fast-food restaurants | 65% | 65% | 65% |
| Pizza | 63 | 64 | 62 |
| Soft drinks | 60 | 61 | 59 |
| Shampoo | 59 | 49 | 69 |
| Toothpaste | 54 | 48 | 60 |
| Ice cream | 53 | 51 | 55 |
| Cereal | 52 | 52 | 53 |
| Antiperspirant/deodorant | 49 | 42 | 56 |
| Potato chips | 45 | 45 | 44 |
| Chewing gum | 45 | 39 | 52 |
| Telephone | 44 | 37 | 51 |
| Juice | 43 | 39 | 48 |
| Hair conditioner | 41 | 21 | 61 |
| Toothbrush | 40 | 36 | 45 |
| Bar soap | 38 | 31 | 45 |
| Camera film | 38 | 26 | 49 |
| Chocolate candy | 31 | 29 | 34 |
| Acne remedy | 31 | 29 | 33 |
| Tortilla chips | 28 | 30 | 26 |

Source: TRU *Teenage Marketing & Lifestyle Study*

most mothers already know what their kids want. Most want to get them what they want for two reasons: first, moms are nice, and second, they don't want to see their purchases go to waste. Without so much as a "gimme," mom often buys the brand of choice. Consequently, the numbers in the consumables table are conservative, with teen girls more influential than teen boys.

Teens also perceive themselves to be highly influential in their families' decisions to purchase durable goods, with about half claiming to influence the purchase of a variety of big-ticket items. In contrast to teens' understated influence over the purchase of consumable goods, qualitative research we've conducted suggests that teens overstate their influence on big-ticket items. While half of teens think they influence the make of car their parents buy, our interviews with teens and parents show that a smaller percentage of parents agree.

Teens do wield considerable influence over the purchase of consumer electronics. Many teens know more about these products than do their parents. Many parents rely on their teenage children for guidance in directing these purchase decisions. Teen influence in the purchase of computers transcends even their role as family expert. Many parents buy multimedia computers primarily because they think their children will benefit.

The 1995 IBM Aptiva advertising featuring actor Paul Reiser effectively sells computers to parents through their children, while getting teens and kids involved in the process. The ads show how the computer is really for kids but also for parents. In other words, it's for the whole family. This plays well to parents, who feel a responsibility to give their children the benefits of a computer. It also motivates kids by showcasing the components that are entertainment oriented (graphics, sound, games, etc.).

# Teen Purchase Influence: Durables

*Although half of teens think they influence the make of car their parents buy, a smaller percentage of parents agree.*

**(percent of teens saying they influence their parents' purchase of selected items, 1994)**

|  | *percent* |
|---|---|
| Vacation/travel | 80% |
| Sports equipment | 78 |
| Magazine subscription | 64 |
| PC software | 64 |
| Personal computer | 63 |
| Home stereo | 57 |
| Car/truck/van | 51 |
| Television | 51 |
| VCR | 50 |

Source: TRU *Teenage Marketing & Lifestyle Study*

As families continue to change and the roles of family members shift, teen influence in the purchasing of durable goods is growing. Marketers of many durable goods should view teens as a primary rather than secondary market. Marketing efforts, when possible, should reflect teens' pronounced role in decision-making. Not only will there be immediate benefits through direct teen purchasing and teen-influenced family purchasing, there may be longer-term pay-offs in brand loyalty.

*Chapter Three*

*Teens and Media*

$T$eens are not only big media users, they're also big media fans. Media help to nationalize the teen experience, connecting teens through common images and expressions. But teens use media differently than do adults or children. Because of this, it's important to understand their media preferences and behaviors.

There's a common misconception about teens and the media. In many of the interviews our staff has with reporters, one of the first questions reporters ask is, "How can advertisers reach teens given that teens are such an elusive media target?" The assumption is that teens are difficult to reach. Reporters rarely ask whether this is true. It isn't. There are many media outlets that reach teens effectively. This misconception keeps some companies from actively targeting teens, even though pursuing them would make strategic sense.

Because teens take cues not only from each other but also from the media, it's important to stay attuned to the media that most influence them. We advise our clients to watch and read the same things teens watch and read. This is a productive way for you to understand teens and, if not stay ahead of them, at least stay even with them. For example, our company subscribes to or gets almost every magazine that influences teens, from *Seventeen*, *YM*, *Sassy*, *'Teen*, and *Teen Beat* to *YSB*, *Vibe*, *Scholastic*, *Rolling Stone*, and *Game Pro*.

When we talk to teens about marketing, we continually are reminded of just how savvy they are, particularly when it comes to discussing and analyzing advertising. In a recent study, we gave teenagers an opportunity to point advertisers toward the best media for reaching them. From a list of 11 choices, we asked teens to recommend the media they thought would be effective in reaching teens and to select the two best.

# Teen-Recommended Media

*Teens strongly recommend radio as
an effective way to reach them.*

**(percent of teens recommending medium as effective in reaching teens
and percent recommending medium as one of two best, 1993)**

| Recommended | *percent* | One of two best | *percent* |
|---|---|---|---|
| Radio | 85% | Radio | 48% |
| Magazines | 75 | Cable TV | 40 |
| Cable TV | 74 | TV (not cable) | 29 |
| Before movies at theater | 68 | Magazines | 26 |
| TV (not cable) | 68 | Before movies at theater | 23 |
| Billboards, scoreboards | 55 | Through the mail | 19 |
| Through the mail | 54 | In school | 11 |
| Sponsored events | 45 | Billboards, scoreboards | 11 |
| In school | 43 | Sponsored events | 11 |
| Newspapers | 40 | Newspapers | 8 |
| Buses, trains, etc. | 30 | Buses, trains, etc. | 5 |

Source: TRU *Teenage Marketing & Lifestyle Study*

## Teens and Radio

Teens strongly recommend radio as an effective way to reach them. This finding may surprise some advertisers, but it makes sense when you consider what radio offers teens. Teens invest a lot of time in listening to the radio. About 95 percent listen to FM radio more than ten hours each week.

To teens, radio means music. Teens' love of music is well documented. Radio programming is almost exclusively comprised, then, of what teens love best. Radio also offers teens a selectivity in music they can't get elsewhere, including MTV. If a researcher had asked my peers and I what type of music we liked when we were teenagers in the late 1960s, we all would have said "rock." Today, teen taste in music is extremely fragmented. Teens might say their favorite music is "rap," "hip hop," "alternative," "metal," "techno," "reggae," or "R&B." A few might even say "country." Radio allows teens to listen to whatever music they prefer.

When we ask teens about local radio, whether in Chicago, Los Angeles, Atlanta, or Tucson, the discussion often becomes heated. Teens are extremely loyal to particular stations. Especially in small towns, radio connects local teenagers, informing them of coming events such as concerts, sports, school events, and so on. Radio also makes celebrities out of local disc jockeys.

Because of the selectivity of radio, it offers efficiency for reaching different teen segments according to ethnic, gender, and geographic characteristics. Because teens are differentiated by their taste in music, the selectivity of radio allows marketers to use different executions for different radio formats.

A teenager who likes rap probably isn't a heavy metal fan and vice versa. A preference for one type of music often excludes other styles. This difference goes far beyond musical preference.

# Favorite Radio Formats of Teens

*Rap is the favorite format of teen boys and
the second favorite of teen girls.*

**(percent of teens mentioning format as one of
their top two favorites, 1994)**

| | *percent* |
|---|---|
| **Boys** | |
| Rap | 34% |
| Hard Rock | 27 |
| Alternative | 23 |
| Top 40 | 22 |
| R&B | 22 |
| **Girls** | |
| Top 40 | 32 |
| Rap | 27 |
| R&B | 27 |
| Country | 27 |
| Alternative | 24 |

Source: TRU *Teenage Marketing & Lifestyle Study*

Teen language, fashion, activities, friends, and attitudes often correlate with taste in music. Understanding this psychographic segmentation, you can communicate in a relevant and appealing way to teen listeners.

Rap is the favorite format of teen boys and the second favorite of teen girls. African-American teens almost exclusively favor rap and R&B stations. White teens also like rap and R&B, and they enjoy alternative, top 40, hard rock, and even classic rock.

## Teens and Magazines

There is no medium as intimate or directly relevant to teenage girls as magazines. Magazines are far more important to teen girls than they are to teen boys. Reflecting this fact, there is a host of magazines specifically directed at teen girls, while currently there is not a single magazine written specifically for teen boys.

Teens' magazine choices indicate what interests them. Girls read for information about fashion, beauty, boys, parents, school, and the future. Boys read for entertainment; they enjoy comics, and they're interested in reading about sports and TV.

Girls rate magazines highly on several levels, and they advise marketers to use magazines to reach them. Perhaps they are savvy enough to realize that magazines are a cost-effective way to target their particular demographic!

With the exception of friends, magazines are the place where most teen girls say they find out about the latest trends. Girls depend on magazines for more than leisure reading. They rely on them to learn about the latest fashions and lifestyle choices and to connect with other girls their age across the country. Girls also "shop" print ads and editorial fashion photos as if they were catalogs.

# Teen Magazine "Bond" Ratings

*Seventeen and YM not only have the largest circulations among teen magazines, but their bond with readers is stronger than that of competitors.*

**(among teens who have read three or four of the last four issues, percent who "strongly" or "somewhat" agree with each statement, 1995)**

|  | Sassy | Seventeen | 'Teen | Teen Beat | YM |
|---|---|---|---|---|---|
| One of my favorites | 65% | 89% | 86% | 67% | 91% |
| Fun to read | 62 | 88 | 85 | 74 | 90 |
| Really trust | 50 | 71 | 67 | 46 | 75 |
| Talk about and share with friends | 44 | 74 | 67 | 57 | 74 |
| Rely for product info | 46 | 61 | 53 | 42 | 59 |
| Read it as soon as I get it | 67 | 85 | 79 | 58 | 84 |

Source: TRU *Teenage Marketing & Lifestyle Study*

*Seventeen* and *YM* are the strongest magazines in the field. They not only have the largest circulations among teen magazines but also their bond with readers is stronger than that of competitors, *'Teen*, *Sassy* , and *Teen Beat*. A few years ago, TRU developed a measure of a magazine's relationship with its readers, which we call "bond" ratings. These bond ratings are important because the closer girls feel to a magazine, the more effective an environment it is for advertisers.

*YM*, which was formerly titled *Young Miss*, has been gaining ground on these measures. Just two years ago it was third, trailing *Seventeen* and *'Teen*.

*'Teen* continues to build a strong circulation, making inroads in the past couple of years by contemporizing its look and image. Its audience remains younger than *YM's* or *Seventeen's*.

*Sassy* is the American relative of the Australian magazine, *Dolly*. *Sassy* is actually a tame version of *Dolly*, reflecting more conservative American attitudes. Even so, *Sassy* made a big splash during its launch in 1987, when Jerry Falwell's Moral Majority criticized it for its frank talk about sex. One article included an illustration of a boy's body, with an arrow pointing to each part and describing its function. Although *Sassy* lost a few advertisers temporarily because of the controversy, Falwell created enough media attention to reach parents and teens. As soon as teens were told to stay away from *Sassy*, they flocked to it. Falwell turned out to be a great *Sassy* circulation marketer. From a profitability perspective, *Sassy* was a disappointment to its former publishers, however. Its third owner, Petersen Publications, which already publishes *'Teen*, now offers package rates for advertising in both *Sassy* and *'Teen*. Sassy's editors are new under Petersen and consequently offer girls a somewhat different "read" than previously, although the new publisher hopes to recapture *Sassy's* original appeal.

In addition to these four strong magazines, there are several others written for teen girls. *Teen Beat* from MacFadden Publications is widely read. The same company (through a merger with Sterling Publications) publishes *Tiger Beat, 16, Teen Machine, SuperTeen, Metal Edge, Black Beat,* and *Right On!*

Competing with *Black Beat* and *Right On!* for African-American teen readers is *YSB* (Young Sisters & Brothers) from Black Entertainment Television (BET).

Competing with *Metal Edge* for the attention of boys who are metal music fans are *Circus* and *Hit Parader*.

Though there are many magazines targeted at teenage girls, older teens are aspirational in their reading. They're moving into magazines like *Cosmopolitan, Glamour, Mademoiselle, and Vogue.*

If you want to reach a dual-audience of teen boys and girls, magazines distributed in high schools can be especially effective. The most successful publisher in this arena is Scholastic Publications, which currently distributes *Science World, Scope, Update, Choices,* and (for younger students) *Junior Scholastic* in the nation's schools. These magazines reach about nine million teens. *Careers & Colleges*, from E. M. Guild, is also distributed in schools. It targets college-bound students twice a year. *Fast Times*, from two California entrepreneurs, is a high-quality publication distributed in history classes.

Reflecting advertisers' increasing interest in the teen market, two major publishers recently launched magazines, without great success. *Tell*, from Hachette, and *Mouth2Mouth*, from Time Publishing Ventures, were pretty slick magazines. Like *Scholastic*, they were designed for both boys and girls. *Tell*, a joint venture between Hachette and NBC, was also an example of a cross-media partnership as a way of reaching more teens. *Tell* looked like a younger version of *US* and found a significant female audience. *Tell* is currently on hold; its most recent issue was published in the fall of 1994. As with all new magazines (*Tell* and *Mouth2Mouth* are good examples) those directed at teens need time to find an audience. And, of course, time is a major investment to publishers.

*Mouth2Mouth* was the vision of its editor-in-chief, Angela Jankow Harrington, whose Hollywood connections and exuberant style fueled the magazine's celebrity focus. Despite keeping its promise to deliver an "in-your-face" information- and celebrity-packed magazine, *Mouth2Mouth* was unable to attract enough teen newsstand buyers or subscribers in its two test issues to convince *Time* to proceed. This was unfortunate, because the magazine found advertising support and high reader interest. Delivering on its editorial promise, however, made it an extremely expensive magazine to publish and that much more of a financial risk.

Nobody has yet created a magazine that is aimed at and appeals to large numbers of teen boys. We can't even begin to count the number of calls we've received in the past 12 years from major publishers and entrepreneurs who, noting the absence of magazines for teen boys, wanted to explore the market. But they all face the same problem: the type of magazine that a lot of boys would pay to read is often a type they cannot sell to an underage audience. *Sassy's* previous publisher experimented with seven issues of a male version, titled *Dirt*, distributing it with *Sassy* and in a polybag with *Marvel* comic books. Without a more direct means of targeting its readers and a greater financial commitment from its publisher, *Dirt* became history.

The most effective way of targeting boys through print is by tapping into the vertical or niche publications that reflect their special interests, such as sports, video games, or music. The

# Top 15 Magazines Read by Teens

*If you want to reach a dual audience of teen boys and girls, magazines distributed in high schools can be especially effective.*

**(percent of teens who read a typical issue of each magazine, by gender, 1994)**

| Boys | percent | Girls | percent |
|---|---|---|---|
| Sports Illustrated | 37% | Seventeen | 46% |
| TV Guide | 30 | YM | 38 |
| Cable Guide | 22 | Teen | 36 |
| Scholastic Network (gross measurement)* | 21 | TV Guide | 36 |
| Game Pro | 19 | Scholastic Network (gross measurement)* | 28 |
| Marvel Comics | 19 | Cable Guide | 24 |
| Sport | 14 | People | 21 |
| Electronic Gaming Monthly | 13 | Reader's Digest | 20 |
| Reader's Digest | 13 | Star and National Enquirer (gross measurement) | 19 |
| Inside Sports | 12 | Sassy | 18 |
| DC Comics | 12 | Glamour | 16 |
| Rolling Stone | 12 | Cosmopolitan | 14 |
| Time | 11 | Mademoiselle | 13 |
| Newsweek | 11 | Soap Opera Digest | 13 |
| People | 11 | Sports Illustrated | 12 |

*includes Science World, Scope, Update, Choices, Jr. Scholastic

Source: TRU *Teenage Marketing & Lifestyle Study*

magazine that enjoys the highest teen male readership is *Sports Illustrated.* Because this is an adult magazine, it is an extremely expensive and inefficient vehicle for targeting teen boys.

## Teens and Broadcast Television

Although there is often much waste in targeting teens through network television, certain programs deliver not only large numbers of teens but also a disproportionately teenaged audience.

With few exceptions, teens' favorite programs are situation comedies. Humor is a key ingredient in programming success with teens. Humor is also key to creating advertising that appeals to this age group. When humor is combined with family situations involving teens, the appeal is even greater.

From "Ozzie & Harriet," "Leave It to Beaver," and "Dobie Gillis," to "The Partridge Family" and "The Brady Bunch," teens have always gravitated toward programming centered on people their own age in family situations. Most of teens' favorite TV shows today likewise focus on families with teenaged children. In the current top-rated programs, the family types range from traditional two-parent families ("Home Improvement") to a single-parent, father-headed household ("Full House") to more cynical views of the American family ("Married with Children" and "The Simpsons"). Regardless of what teens think about their own families, family is the core of teen life. Teens like to watch other families (real or fictional) to gain a perspective on their own experience.

The single most important network program for teens in the past ten years is not a sitcom. It does, however, incorporate family situations. "Beverly Hills, 90210" has been the favorite program of teen girls since it debuted three years ago. It's rare for one television show to sustain this level of popularity for so long.

At one time, nearly half of teen girls said that "90210" was one of their three favorite programs. Its popularity has since declined by half, but it still remains girls' favorite show.

Boys also watch "90210" in fairly big numbers. When we ask them about the show, they tell us it's not cool to admit they watch the show, "but you gotta see what the girls are watching." I don't think they are being entirely honest; they probably like the show regardless of what girls are watching.

## Teens and Cable Television

MTV is the most-watched cable channel by teenagers. It's often on the cutting edge of what's popular not only in music but also in teen and young adult culture and lifestyle. MTV is also successfully appealing to teens with its nonmusical programming, such as "MTV Sports" and "Beavis & Butt-Head." Seven percent of teen boys name "Beavis & Butt-Head" as one of their favorite shows.

These days there is less "M" in MTV and more traditional "TV," if "Beavis & Butt-head" can be considered traditional. MTV now incorporates news, sports, comedy, drama, and other programming into its schedule. While many of the teens we talk to who are music aficionados (most of whom are boys) miss MTV's former emphasis on music videos, the current format probably has made MTV more important as a cultural touchstone for teens and young adults.

MTV faces a programming problem: appealing to teens' increasingly fragmented musical tastes. While radio can target its programming to distinctive musical preferences, MTV must rotate between mainstream rock, metal, rap, and R&B. Someday, if we ever have 500 cable channels, maybe there will be an MTV Rap, MTV Metal, and so on.

# Teens' Favorite Cable Networks

*MTV is the cable channel most watched by teenagers.*

**(average hours teens view weekly, by gender, 1994)**

|  | *hours* |
|---|---|
| **Boys** | |
| MTV | 5.3 |
| ESPN | 5.2 |
| USA | 3.5 |
| **Girls** | |
| MTV | 5.1 |
| USA | 3.0 |
| VH-1 | 2.7 |

Source: TRU *Teenage Marketing & Lifestyle Study*

As influential as MTV is to the overall teen market, African-American teens spend more time viewing BET (Black Entertainment Television), whose programming mix is fairly similar to MTV's. Because African-American teens are on the forefront of teen trends, BET's influence is considerable.

ESPN is another important vehicle for reaching teens. Teen boys spend almost as much time watching ESPN as MTV. With ESPN taking a leadership role in sports programming, including more non-game programs, teen boys have become bigger fans of this network.

Although its audience is small compared to MTV's, The Box is another extremely influential cable network. A sort of pay-per-view jukebox, this network is closely monitored by record labels for cues to who's new and hot. Rap and hip-hop dominate air play on The Box.

## Teens and Newspapers

Considering all the talk about the weakness of newsprint in the face of the increasing number of electronic and interactive media, it may surprise many marketers to discover that 84 percent of teen boys and 80 percent of teen girls look at a newspaper each week. Certainly it's surprising to know that as many teen boys as girls read newspapers, though this can be explained in part by the fact that many boys are simply glancing at the box score from yesterday's game. But other teens evidently spend considerable time reading newspapers. Boys spend 3.7 hours reading a newspaper during an average week, while girls spend 3.0 hours, which amounts to average daily newspaper doses of a little more than half an hour for boys and somewhat less for girls.

Newspapers can be a viable medium with which to reach teens for several reasons. First, school newspapers enjoy a special

# Teens' Favorite Newspaper Sections

*Eighty-four percent of teen boys and 80 percent of teen girls look at a newspaper each week.*

**(percent of teens selecting newspaper section as their favorite, by gender, 1994)**

|  | *percent* |
|---|---|
| **Boys** | |
| Sports | 61% |
| Comics | 56 |
| Entertainment | 20 |
| News | 19 |
| **Girls** | |
| Comics | 51 |
| Horoscope | 36 |
| Entertainment | 20 |
| News | 19 |

Source: TRU *Teenage Marketing & Lifestyle Study*

bond with their readers. Second, more major dailies are beginning regular teen sections. In fact, *Parade* will soon publish a teen supplement titled *React*. Cokie Dishon, who premiered the *Chicago Tribune's Kid News*, is also responsible for *React*. Third, for heavier-reading teens, newspapers provide a convenient, daily source of information and entertainment.

## Other Media Outlets

In addition to traditional media, you can reach teens through alternative or place-based media. In our *Teenage Marketing & Lifestyle Study*, we ask teens which alternative media they have seen and which they like.

The results of this measure are revealing. Exposure to alternative media does not necessarily equate to likability, though there is some correlation. Advertising before movies ranks first on exposure and second on likability. While many adults find advertising at theaters annoying, or even an infringement on their time (after all, they paid to be there), teens view it as "bonus" entertainment. The ads shown at theaters often are highly original, because advertisers understand that, to be effective, theater ads must have greater production and entertainment value than television ads.

More than 80 percent of teens have received advertising through the mail, but only one-third like it. In our syndicated study, only 19 percent of teens recommend "through the mail" as one of the two best ways to reach them.

We recently conducted a spring-break research project among college students at a couple of their favorite destinations: South Padre Island in Texas and Lake Havasu in Arizona. Spring break represents a marketing opportunity, with many companies distributing samples of their products. College students

# Teens and Alternative Media

*Teens view advertising at theaters as "bonus" entertainment.*

**(percent of teens who have seen medium and percent who like medium, 1993)**

|  | alternative media | |
|  | seen | like |
|---|---|---|
| Before movie/theater | 92% | 56% |
| Before movie/video | 99 | 45 |
| Billboards | 88 | 56 |
| Mail | 86 | 38 |
| Free product samples | 82 | 68 |
| Grocery card/shelf | 77 | 32 |
| Sponsored events | 75 | 49 |
| Scoreboards | 67 | 42 |
| Posters at school | 63 | 38 |
| School newspaper | 52 | 36 |
| TV news at school | 46 | 35 |
| Classroom materials | 42 | 24 |

Source: TRU *Teenage Marketing & Lifestyle Study*

embrace what's free. In fact, at Padre Island, a common spring-break chant was, "Free shit! Free shit! Free shit!" This perhaps explains why teens' favorite alternative advertising is product sampling. They love getting something for nothing. Yet about one in five teens has never received a free product sample.

Probably the best-known place-based advertising vehicle directed at teens is "Channel One," a daily news program sent by satellite into many of the nation's middle and high schools. Whittle Communications launched "Channel One" several years ago amid much controversy because 2 of its 12 minutes a day are composed of advertising. Those who object to "Channel One" argue that advertising does not belong in the schools, especially shown to a captive audience. But advertising has long been in the schools, from space advertising in *Scholastic* or school newspapers to corporate-sponsored promotions, such as the Campbell Soup label program in elementary school. "Channel One" set off the critics because of the high impact of television advertising and the belief that students would be force-fed commercials as part of their classroom lessons.

Our position is that "Channel One" is sound programming. It makes news relevant to kids. Its coverage of the fall of the Berlin Wall, for example, opened the eyes of thousands of American teens. Furthermore, teens are bombarded with hundreds of advertising messages every day. Because advertising has become so much a part of their lives, they are quite adept at tuning it in or out. To some, this point alone might not justify in-school TV advertising, but in combination with the quality of the program, we feel comfortable recommending "Channel One" to advertisers. Another plus for the schools is that "Channel One" gives VCRs and televisions to schools that air its programming.

The partnership between corporate America and the country's schools should be viewed cautiously but with an open mind. With educational resources shrinking to the point that some schools are using history books published 30 years ago, corporate funding of educational programs and materials has become more prevalent, more necessary, and more attractive. European countries have long been more open to corporate funding for educators than the United States, believing the materials and programs the schools receive are well worth the price of exposing students to a corporate logo or an advertising message.

Modern Talking Pictures is one company that makes its living by developing and executing corporate-educational partnerships. It has worked with a variety of brands, giving them exposure to students and giving the schools worthwhile programs.

Other media companies also place advertising in schools. American Passage Marketing Corporation targets high school students with GymBoards in school locker rooms. Each board is customized with the names and colors of the school team as well as advertising. This program is particularly attractive because it allows advertisers to target teenage boys and girls separately. Another company, Market Source, places high-tech wall boards, called the High School Source, in schools. In addition to space for advertising, the boards include customized monthly calendars of school events and a moving LED message, programmed by schools for announcements.

*Chapter Four*

*Teen Activities and Interests*

What teenagers do with their leisure time segments them, profiles them, and offers opportunities to marketers. So much of what teenagers are is what they do. They tend to choose their friends based on shared interests. That's why teens who are into basketball hang out together, as do those who volunteer, work on cars, create music, go to the mall, or even do drugs. Teens look for and gravitate toward others who are like them. Their interests and activities can make for an instant bond.

Understanding what teens do and when they do it is key to creating relevant advertising for teenagers and reaching them when they're ready to receive your messages.

Teens still participate in and favor many of the activities they always have, from watching TV to dancing. They're also computing on-line, going to religious functions, and cooking. In fact, many teen leisure-time activities are also those that are enjoyed by the rest of the population.

Often, the activities that the largest numbers of teens take part in are also those teens spend the most time doing. During the week, more teens are likely to watch TV than take part in any other leisure-time activity. They also spend more time watching TV (11.5 hours) than they spend in any other activity.

Some activities have high participation levels, yet teens spend little time engaged in the activity. Seventy-six percent of teens read a newspaper during the past week, but they spent only 2.8 hours doing so.

Recognizing the difference between teen participation and involvement (time spent doing it) is important if you want to promotionally tie into or depict an activity in advertising. When choosing an activity for use in teen-directed marketing and advertising, consider not only the size of the teen audience but also teens' level of involvement.

Today's teens are busier than ever, engaging in a greater variety of activities than teens did in the past. Still, we constantly hear teens exclaim, "Life is boring." And they tell us that the age-old parent-teen dialogue can still be heard in households across the country:

"Where are you going?"

*"Out."*

"What are you going to do?"

*"Nothing."*

Although teen fashions, music, and lifestyles change, there are constants in teens' leisure activities. In many ways, the teen years are a time of learning about limits, of learning to make decisions, and of learning how to be responsible for one's time. Teen activities can be grouped according to whether the activities are self-directed or externally imposed.

We divide teen leisure-time activities into three groups based on their motivations. Group 1 activities are those that teens choose to do and think are fun (e.g., dancing, hanging out, going to movies and concerts). Group 2 activities are those that teens choose to do because they are good for them physically, intellectually, or morally (e.g., working out, going to the library, volunteering). Group 3 activities are those that someone else says the teen must do (e.g., running errands, cleaning the house, taking care of a sibling, studying). Of the 51 activities measured by TRU, 58 percent fall into the "I choose/it's fun" group. Twenty-one percent are "I choose/good for me" activities, while an additional 21 percent are "someone else chooses/gotta do" types of activities.

In part by design, most of the activities TRU measures come under the heading of "I choose/it's fun." These are leisure-time

# Leisure-Time Activities of Teens

*Many teen leisure-time activities are also those enjoyed by the rest of the population.*

**(percent of teenagers participating in selected activities during the past week, and number of hours teens spent participating in the activity, 1994)**

|  | percent participating | number of hours |
|---|---|---|
| Watching TV | 98% | 11.5 |
| Listening to FM radio | 95 | 10.3 |
| Listening to CDs, tapes, records | 93 | 9.6 |
| Talking on phone (local calls) | 81 | 6.2 |
| "Hanging out" with friends | 80 | 8.0 |
| Using a microwave oven | 80 | 4.7 |
| Eating fast food | 79 | 3.9 |
| Reading newspapers | 76 | 2.8 |
| Playing sports | 75 | 6.6 |
| Reading magazines for pleasure | 73 | 2.7 |
| Exercising/working out | 72 | 5.0 |
| Cleaning the house | 72 | 3.6 |
| Cooking/preparing meals for self | 71 | 2.9 |
| Watching rented videos | 69 | 4.2 |
| Shopping for self | 62 | 3.0 |
| Reading books for pleasure | 60 | 4.5 |
| Caring for/playing with children | 58 | 4.2 |
| Working on a hobby | 56 | 3.6 |
| Studying | 55 | 3.8 |
| "Cruising" in car | 53 | 3.9 |
| Running errands for family | 52 | 2.3 |

Source: TRU *Teenage Marketing & Lifestyle Study*

*(continued)*

*(continued from previous page)*

|  | percent participating | number of hours |
|---|---|---|
| Doing laundry | 51% | 2.3 |
| Shopping at/hanging out at mall | 50 | 2.7 |
| Going to parties | 49 | 3.2 |
| Driving a car | 49 | 4.3 |
| Going to religious functions | 48 | 2.6 |
| Dating/being with boyfriend/girlfriend | 48 | 5.0 |
| Going to movie theaters | 48 | 2.2 |
| Cooking/preparing meals for family | 47 | 2.1 |
| Playing home videogames | 46 | 3.0 |
| Talking on phone (long distance) | 45 | 2.1 |
| Grocery shopping for family | 44 | 1.9 |
| Going to sports events | 41 | 2.5 |
| Baking | 37 | 1.6 |
| Using a computer at home | 37 | 2.3 |
| Using a computer at school/elsewhere | 36 | 1.9 |
| Working at a regular paid job | 34 | 5.1 |
| Going to a library/museum/gallery | 33 | 1.4 |
| Playing computer games | 33 | 1.7 |
| Going to amusement/ theme park | 32 | 2.1 |
| Playing board games | 31 | 1.2 |
| Going dancing | 29 | 1.5 |
| Playing a musical instrument | 27 | 2.0 |
| Doing volunteer work | 24 | 1.3 |
| Playing arcade videogames | 24 | 1.2 |
| Reading magazines for school | 22 | 0.8 |
| Listening to AM radio | 20 | 1.0 |
| Going to concerts | 20 | 1.1 |
| Working on a car/truck/motorcycle | 17 | 1.1 |
| Going to community centers/YMCA | 15 | 1.0 |
| Using an on-line computer service | 12 | 0.6 |

Source: TRU *Teenage Marketing & Lifestyle Study*

activities over which teens have significant control. If you incorporate "I choose/it's fun" activities into your advertising and promotional messages, your brand can benefit from the halo effect of a good time.

Teens also pursue activities of their own choosing for reasons of self-improvement or social benefit. Many teens need to feel that they make a difference in the world. You can help teens raise their profile as contributors to the common good. By doing so, you send a message to teens that their spending and brand choices are important and have an impact beyond the sale in a way that is uniquely theirs. This is not to say, however, that teens are willing to spend more for a product just because a percentage of the sale is donated to a popular cause. But, if all else is equal, such a tie-in can make a difference.

## The Importance of Socializing

Perhaps there is no activity more important to teens from an emotional, psychological, and even marketing sense than socializing. Socializing includes hanging out with friends, cruising, dating, partying, even meeting in cyberspace. But teens socialize differently than in the recent past. When we first measured "cruising" 12 years ago, for example, it was predominantly a male activity. Now girls are just as likely to cruise in cars, showing how much more independent and socially proactive girls have become in the last decade.

Dating has especially evolved, both in high school and on college campuses. Today, boys and girls become friends before pairing off. Formal dating is rarer than it was 10 and 20 years ago, while group dating is more the norm. In focus groups about this topic, teen girls tell us that they seldom wait around for boys to ask them out on a date, and they might be put off if a boy did ask

# High-Participation/ High-Involvement Activities

*During the week, more teens are likely to watch TV than take part in any other leisure-time activity.*

**(activities in which a large percentage of teenagers participated during the past week and in which teens spent a lot of time participating, 1994)**

|  | spent a lot of time participating | |
|---|---|---|
|  | percent participating | number of hours |
| Watching TV | 98% | 11.5 |
| Listening to FM radio | 95 | 10.3 |
| Listening to CDs, tapes, records | 93 | 9.6 |
| Hanging out with friends | 80 | 8.0 |
| Playing sports | 75 | 6.6 |

Source: TRU *Teenage Marketing & Lifestyle Study*

# High-Participation/ Low-Involvement Activities

*Seventy-six percent of teens read a newspaper during the past week, but they spent only 2.8 hours doing so.*

**(activities in which a large percentage of teenagers participated during the past week but in which teens spent little time participating, 1994)**

|  | spent little time participating | |
|---|---|---|
|  | *percent participating* | *number of hours* |
| Eating fast food | 79% | 3.9 |
| Reading newspapers | 76 | 2.8 |
| Using a microwave oven | 80 | 4.7 |
| Reading magazines for pleasure | 73 | 2.7 |
| Cooking/preparing meals for self | 71 | 2.9 |

Source: TRU *Teenage Marketing & Lifestyle Study*

them out. When we asked a group of 16-year-old girls how they would react if a guy "they only kind of knew" called them up and asked them out, they exclaimed, "That would be just too weird!"

Instead, couples are finding each other within a group of mixed-gender friends—certainly a positive sociological shift. But there's no question about it: teens still yearn to have a boyfriend or girlfriend. Only the means to the end have changed. Boyfriends and girlfriends typically become friends first.

Of course, not all teens socialize to the same extent, and the frequency with which they socialize correlates not only with age, but also with self-esteem. When you're accepted by and become part of a group that regularly congregates and communicates, you feel better about yourself.

We asked our national sample of teens the following question: "How many nights a week do you usually ... stay at home (without friends) ... date/be with boyfriend/girlfriend ... get together with friends?" The data show that nearly nine out of ten teens spend at least one evening by themselves at home during the week, and they spend at least one evening with friends. Only about half spend at least one evening a week with a boyfriend or girlfriend.

Girls spend more nights a week out on dates than boys do. One reason for this is that teen girls often date older boys, and older teens spend more evenings out with friends or with boyfriends/girlfriends than do younger teens. Boys aren't as aspirational when it comes to dating.

## Where Teens Spend Their Free Time

Recently, we were conducting focus groups to expose teens to some preliminary advertising ideas for a top brand. The storyboards depicted teens heading to a movie theater after

# What Teens Do During the Week

*Nearly nine out of ten teens spend at least one evening by themselves at home during the week, and they spend at least one evening with friends.*

**(percent of teens participating in activity at least one evening a week and average number of evenings spent participating in activity during a week, by gender and age, 1994)**

| | gender | | | | | |
| | total | | boys | | girls | |
| | % | no. | % | no. | % | no. |
|---|---|---|---|---|---|---|
| Stay at home (without friends) | 89% | 3 | 87% | 3 | 91% | 3 |
| Get together with friends | 88 | 3 | 86 | 3 | 90 | 3 |
| Date/be with boyfriend/ girlfriend | 49 | 2 | 44 | 1 | 55 | 2 |

| | age | | | | | |
| | 12-15 | | 16-17 | | 18-19 | |
| | % | no. | % | no. | % | no. |
|---|---|---|---|---|---|---|
| Stay at home (without friends) | 91% | 4 | 88% | 3 | 86% | 3 |
| Get together with friends | 86 | 3 | 89 | 3 | 92 | 3 |
| Date/be with boyfriend/ girlfriend | 39 | 1 | 59 | 2 | 63 | 2 |

Source: TRU *Teenage Marketing & Lifestyle Study*

school. This was an instant "disconnect" to respondents. Several said, "Hey, we don't go to movies after school. That just doesn't make sense." Once teens disconnect from an ad, it's almost impossible to get them back. So, something as seemingly innocuous as an afternoon movie can spell trouble for an otherwise strong message.

This may be an obvious example of an activity that does not match the occasion. But it led us to develop a measure to determine which teen venues are appropriate for which occasions. Do teens do the same things after school as they do on weekends? Do they go to different places when on a date than they would if they were hanging out with friends?

We presented our national teen sample with a list of activities and asked them to identify those in which they participate after school, on weekends, and on a date (or, more simply, with a girlfriend or boyfriend).

As expected, the findings show that teens frequent different places at different times. Nearly two-thirds spend their free time after school at home, while only about one-third spend their free time on weekends at home, and only 1 in 20 stay home during a date. The top three places teens go after school are home, or to a friend's house, or they remain at or near school to take part in sports or other activities. On weekends, teens are most likely to be at a friend's house, to go to a party, or to hang out at a mall. On a date, teens are most likely to go to a movie, to a restaurant, or to a friend's house.

Teens frequent the widest variety of places on weekends, as shown by the double-digit levels on all but one measured place—school. On dates, teens are surprisingly traditional; they go to movies, restaurants, their boyfriend's or girlfriend's house, or a

# Where Teens Prefer to Spend Their Leisure Time

*Nearly two-thirds of teens prefer to spend their free time after school at home.*

(percent of teens saying they prefer to spend their leisure time at selected places after school, on weekends, and on a date; respondents could pick up to three places, 1994)

| | prefer to spend leisure time | | |
| --- | --- | --- | --- |
| | after school | weekend | on a date* |
| Home | 63% | 30% | 6% |
| Friend's house | 55 | 52 | 6 |
| School/around school | 30 | 7 | 2 |
| Sporting facility | 28 | 25 | 4 |
| Boyfriend's/girlfriend's house | 26 | 34 | 36 |
| School dances | 18 | 20 | 17 |
| Mall | 17 | 44 | 11 |
| Downtown/uptown/city | 17 | 32 | 14 |
| Video arcade | 16 | 23 | 4 |
| Restaurant | 16 | 32 | 36 |
| Park | 15 | 28 | 17 |
| Party | 8 | 48 | 26 |
| Bowling alley | 8 | 22 | 9 |
| Movie theater | 8 | 43 | 55 |
| Church/place of worship | 8 | 36 | 2 |
| Roller rink | 7 | 24 | 9 |
| Teen/dance clubs | 7 | 23 | 15 |
| Beach | 7 | 39 | 13 |
| Concerts | 4 | 26 | 18 |

*those who said they date/get together with their boyfriend or girlfriend at least once a week

Source: TRU *Teenage Marketing & Lifestyle Study*

party. Although dating has evolved, teens still go to the same places on dates.

One intriguing finding is that except for leisure time after school, teens prefer to spend their free time at someone else's home! On weekends, they say they get together with a friend but not at their own home. When they date, they say they go to their boyfriend's or girlfriend's home, but again not to their own. This is another life-stage truth. Most teens have at least one friend who has a "party" house. Usually, it's a friend whose parents aren't home, or, as teens tell us, whose parents "don't care." Although parents admonish their children when they're young not to behave in someone else's home differently than they are expected to behave in their own home, when kids become teens they look for friends' homes where they can do just that.

Another interesting pattern in the data is that girls frequent a broader range of venues than do boys. With the exception of sporting facilities and video arcades, significantly more girls than boys spend time at each of the listed venues, regardless of occasion.

In general, younger teens (aged 12 to 15) prefer to spend their free time at places requiring little planning or travel, such as the mall, movies, roller rinks, video arcades, or school (for school-sponsored activities). Older teens, particularly 16- and 17-year-olds, enjoy the widest variety of venues, including restaurants, a friend's house, the city, concerts, parties, and teen/dance clubs. These are the teens for whom a car (their own or a friend's) means new-found independence and empowerment.

Now that you know what teens like to do when, you can incorporate this information into your advertising. As stated at the outset, if you miss the mark with teens even by a small margin, you've probably missed it entirely.

# Where Teens Prefer to Spend Their Leisure Time, by Gender

*Girls prefer to frequent a broader range*
*of venues than do boys.*

**(percent of teens saying they prefer to spend their leisure time at selected places after school, on weekends, and on a date, by gender, 1994)**

|  | boys | girls |
|---|---|---|
| **AFTER SCHOOL** | | |
| **Preferred by more girls** | | |
| School/around school | 25% | 35% |
| Boyfriend's/girlfriend's house | 22 | 30 |
| School dances | 16 | 21 |
| The mall | 15 | 20 |
| **Preferred by more boys** | | |
| Sporting facility | 31 | 25 |
| Video arcade | 19 | 12 |
| **ON WEEKENDS** | | |
| **Preferred by more girls** | | |
| Party | 45 | 2 |
| The mall | 40 | 49 |
| Movie theater | 40 | 46 |
| Beach | 36 | 42 |
| Boyfriend's/girlfriend's house | 31 | 38 |
| Restaurant | 29 | 35 |
| Roller rink | 21 | 26 |
| Teen/dance clubs | 18 | 28 |
| **Preferred by more boys** | | |
| Video arcade | 28 | 18 |
| **ON A DATE** | | |
| **Preferred by more girls** | | |
| Movie theater | 47 | 54 |
| Restaurant | 34 | 38 |
| Concerts | 15 | 20 |

Source: TRU *Teenage Marketing & Lifestyle Study*

## Sports and Recreational Activities

After music, nothing unites teens more than sports. Sports participation and interest is at an all-time high for both teen boys and girls. Sports are a natural for teen promotions and advertising.

Nearly three-quarters of teens play sports in a given week, including two-thirds of girls. More than 40 percent of both boys and girls attend sports events in a given week. Further, more than 80 percent of boys and girls say that high-school sports, college sports, and pro sports are "in." Eighty percent also say that being on a school sports team is "in." The jock stigma that characterized athletic participation in the late 1960s and early 1970s is long gone.

It's not just a certain type of individual who's into sports today. It's almost everybody. We see it every time we do a focus group. Typically, about half the boys are wearing baseball caps and about equal numbers of boys and girls are wearing either college or pro-sports team jerseys, sweats, or jackets. And, of course, most teens wear athletic shoes (although lately more are wearing boots). We're seeing a unisex style in how teens dress, and sports apparel contributes greatly to this trend.

In the warm-up to group discussions, when we ask participants to say what they would be doing if they weren't at the focus group, they respond with "playing sports."

TRU measures teen participation in 42 sports, from baseball to surfing, in our syndicated study. Our clients use this information to decide which sports to tie into when advertising or promoting to teenagers. We ask teens to rank sports by their level of participation outside of school (in other words, sports of their choice rather than school imposed) in the past year, and whether a sport is one of their three favorites. Although boys and girls are

# Teen Boys: Sports Participation and Favorite Sports

*Basketball is by far the most popular sport with boys.*

**(rank order of sports in which teen boys participated in the past year and sports that are one of teen boys' three favorites, 1994)**

| participated in past 12 months | one of three favorites |
|---|---|
| 1. Basketball | 1. Basketball |
| 2. Swimming | 2. Baseball |
| 3. Football | 3. Football |
| 4. Baseball | 4. Swimming |
| 5. Billiards/pool | 5. Bicycling |
| 6. Bicycling | 6. Billiards/pool |

Source: TRU *Teenage Marketing & Lifestyle Study*

# Teen Girls: Sports Participation and Favorite Sports

*Swimming is the most popular sport with girls.*

**(rank order of sports in which teen girls participated in the past year and sports that are one of teen girls' three favorites, 1994)**

| participated in past 12 months | one of three favorites |
|---|---|
| 1. Swimming | 1. Swimming |
| 2. Exercise/aerobics | 2. Volleyball |
| 3. Jogging/running | 3. Basketball |
| 4. Basketball | 4. Softball |
| 5. Bicycling | 5. Exercise/aerobics |
| 6. Volleyball | 6. Bicycling |

Source: TRU *Teenage Marketing & Lifestyle Study*

both highly involved in sports, the sports they participate in and favor differ.

Teens' favorite sports are not necessarily the ones in which they are most likely to participate. Teens face financial, geographic, and other obstacles to their participation in certain sports. Golfing and skiing are expensive, for example. Snowboarding requires mountains, while surfing requires an ocean. Additionally, teens may participate in a sport for reasons of health or because their friends pressure them into it, but they may not enjoy it all that much.

Basketball is by far the most-popular sport with boys. It's the sport with the highest participation rate and the one most-mentioned as a favorite. Basketball is the third-most popular sport among girls (after swimming and volleyball). Not surprisingly, the NBA has been the most successful of the major pro-sports leagues at marketing its players and product, yielding the majority of teens' favorite professional athletes.

Unlike basketball, which appeals to both boys and girls, many sports are preferred significantly more by one gender. Steer clear of these sports if you want to advertise or promote to a dual-gender audience.

The following responses from focus group participants reveal the differences in how boys and girls approach sports:

"More guys play sports for fun than girls. They're more spontaneous about playing. We'll play, like in the summer, if we're all at someone's house and they happen to have a basketball net."—*16-year-old girl*

"Everybody plays sports now, so there really aren't jocks anymore. Except for the three-sport kind of guy." —*17-year-old boy*

# Single-Gender Sports

*If you want to advertise or promote to a dual-gender audience, steer clear of sports preferred significantly more by one gender*

**(among sports that are favored by one gender significantly more than the other, percent of boys and girls citing sport as one of three favorites, 1994)**

|  | *boys* | *girls* |
|---|---|---|
| **Preferred by boys** | | |
| Football | 26% | 7% |
| Weight training | 15 | 5 |
| Fishing | 15 | 6 |
| Hunting | 9 | 1 |
| Golf | 7 | 2 |
| **Preferred by girls** | | |
| Swimming | 19 | 43 |
| Volleyball | 8 | 23 |
| Exercise/Aerobics | 4 | 19 |
| Horseback riding | 3 | 10 |
| Roller skating | 3 | 10 |
| Gymnastics | 1 | 8 |

Source: TRU *Teenage Marketing & Lifestyle Study*

"For girls, sports means more aerobics and exercise. We'll all go to a health club and work out."—*16-year-old girl*

"Sports are plain cool. Everybody likes them and wants to be at them."—*14-year-old male*

When deciding which sport to tie into with a promotion or to use thematically or executionally in advertising, consider both behavior (participation) and attitude (a favorite). To gain a better understanding of teen attitudes toward sports, TRU developed the Sports Affinity Index. This index reveals the sports that enjoy an extraordinary level of enthusiasm among those who participate in them. The Teen Sports Affinity Index is based on the percentage of teens participating in a sport who also name the sport as one of their three favorites. A perfect score would be 100, meaning that all participants name the sport as one of their favorites.

By using the percent participating in the sport as the base for the calculation, the index picks up emerging sports: those with low levels of participation but which are hugely popular among participants. By tying into these popular alternative sports, you can separate your company from the many others that portray traditional mass-participation sports in their teen marketing. The thinking is that teens can be attracted vicariously to certain sports in which they may not have the opportunity (again, because of the expense, geography, etc.) to participate. Sports with a high Affinity Index transcend participation numbers. They excite teens, grab their attention, and offer something special.

The rank-order of the index differs from the previous sport list. Three of girls' top sports are water sports. In contrast, boys' top water sport is water skiing at number 11. With the exception of weight training among boys, exercise-oriented sports have low indices, meaning that although many teens participate in

# Teen Sports Affinity Index

*Sports with a high Affinity Index excite teens, grab their attention, and offer something special.*

**(Teen Sports Affinity Index by gender, 1994; the Teen Sports Affinity Index is calculated by multiplying the percent of teen boys or girls who participate in a sport by the proportion who rank the sport as one of their three favorites)**

### *Teen Boys' Sports Affinity Index*

| | | | |
|---|---|---|---|
| Basketball | 58 | Snowboarding | 29 |
| Baseball | 54 | Scuba diving | 29 |
| Dirt motorcycling | 50 | Gymnastics | 29* |
| Football | 48 | Camping/hiking | 28 |
| Hunting | 45 | Mountain climbing/ | |
| Downhill skiing | 38 | rappelling | 27 |
| Weight training | 38 | Skateboarding | 27 |
| Wrestling | 38 | Golf | 27 |
| Soccer | 36 | Surfing | 23* |
| Sailboarding | 36* | Tennis | 23 |
| Water skiing | 36 | Roller skating | 22 |
| Hockey | 36 | Snowmobiling | 22 |
| Hot-rodding | 35 | Volleyball | 21 |
| Fishing | 34 | Cross-country skiing | 21 |
| Boxing | 33 | Sailing | 18 |
| Swimming | 32 | Handball | 17 |
| Bicycling | 32 | Bowling | 16 |
| Motocross | 31* | Ice skating | 14 |
| Billiards/pool | 31 | Jogging/running | 14 |
| Track & field | 31 | Racquetball | 12 |
| Horseback riding | 31 | Exercise/aerobics | 12 |
| In-line skating | 29 | | |

*\*Number of participants is too few to assure reliability of index for this sport.*
Source: TRU *Teenage Marketing & Lifestyle Study*

*(continued)*

*(continued from previous page)*

### Teen Girls' Sports Affinity Index

| | | | |
|---|---|---|---|
| Swimming | 64 | Bowling | 30 |
| Horseback riding | 57 | Weight training | 30 |
| Softball | 52 | Sailing | 29 |
| Downhill skiing | 51 | Wrestling | 27 |
| Gymnastics | 51 | Ice skating | 25 |
| Volleyball | 49 | Fishing | 24 |
| Scuba diving | 46* | Hunting | 24* |
| Basketball | 44 | Boxing | 23* |
| Water skiing | 39 | Cross-country skiing | 23* |
| Dirt motorcycling | 39* | Surfing | 22* |
| Track & field | 38 | Snowmobiling | 22 |
| Billiards/pool | 37 | Mountain climbing/ | |
| Tennis | 35 | rappelling | 20 |
| In-line skating | 34 | Racquetball | 20 |
| Football | 34 | Snowboarding | 19* |
| Soccer | 33 | Skateboarding | 18 |
| Camping/hiking | 33 | Sailboarding | 17* |
| Roller skating | 31 | Jogging/running | 17 |
| Exercise/aerobics | 31 | Handball | 15 |
| Bicycling | 31 | Golf | 15 |
| Hockey | 31 | Motocross | 12 |
| Hot-rodding | 30* | | |

*Number of participants is too few to assure reliability of index for this sport.*
Source: TRU *Teenage Marketing & Lifestyle Study*

them, few consider them favorites. Sports such as skiing, sailboarding, dirt biking, hot-rodding, and horseback riding have low participation levels, but the teens who participate in them do so enthusiastically. These adrenaline-producing, heart-thumping sports emerge with high scores on the Affinity Index. They offer you an opportunity to associate your brand with a sport that's new and exciting. If you watch ESPN2 and MTV Sports, you'll see a variety of sport hybrids—what teens refer to as "extreme" or "radical" sports—that you can link to your brand. Mountain Dew, for one, has effectively connected its brand image to rugged, outdoor, high-energy sports.

Still, baseball/softball and basketball, two of the most heavily participated-in sports, have high indices among both girls and boys. Based on the Teen Sports Affinity Index, basketball, baseball/softball, and downhill skiing are the sports with the strongest appeal for boys and girls combined. For boys only, you should consider football and a few of the individual sports like dirt biking and sailboarding. For girls only, swimming, horseback riding, gymnastics, and volleyball are the best candidates.

*Chapter Five*

*Teen Trends and Social Hierarchy*

There's probably no segment of the population as involved in or motivated by lifestyle trends as teenagers. From the latest in language and music to fashion and "what to do," teens are searching for and influenced by what is new and hot.

When adults think about teens, they often focus on teenagers' fascination with fads and trends. Reporters frequently ask TRU, "What's the latest teen trend?" Staying attuned to teen trends is a challenge for marketers, and it's one of the most interesting aspects of teen lives.

We help marketers identify what's current in teen lifestyles by probing what's in and what's out in our twice-yearly syndicated study. With teens, even twice a year may not be enough to keep up with their "in" and "out" lists, because teen fads can change overnight.

To get a jump on the latest trends, you need to look where teens look. In our syndicated study, we ask teens to name the one or two sources they most rely on for the latest trends.

Teens struggle with and are highly influenced by peer pressure. It should come as no surprise, then, that teens rate friends (47 percent) as the most important source for new trends. Another 13 percent say they learn about trends from the "coolest" people at school, while 4 percent learn about trends from the "weirdest." Overall, 55 percent of teens cite peers as the source for new trends. There are no significant gender or racial differences in these responses.

The message is clear: some of the best teen research costs nothing. Observe! Go where teens go. Watch them, listen to them, see what they do and how they do it.

Now that you know how influential friends are, the logical next question is, where do their friends learn about trends? The answer is, they learn about trends from a combination of sources, most of them forms of entertainment or media. The second most important trend source is magazines. Magazines rate highly because of girls: twice as many girls as boys name magazines as one of the two best places for finding out about trends. What's more, almost as many girls select magazines as select friends. Several strong magazines are directed specifically at teen girls. From *Seventeen* and *YM*, to fashion magazines, such as *Vogue* and *Cosmopolitan*, teenage girls depend on these publications for information about fashion, beauty, and boys. Teen boys, on the other hand, don't have any regularly published magazines directed exclusively at them.

TV is the third most-frequently named source of trend information for both boys and girls. If you're a TV fan, you've noticed the proliferation of new TV programs with a noticeable teen appeal. Adding to TV's importance in fueling trends is the fact that television is such a big part of everyday life. The frequency of television viewing by itself makes TV an influential source of trend information.

Nineteen percent of all teens and 32 percent of African-American teens name music videos (which TRU measures separately from TV) as one of the two most influential sources for finding out about new trends. To African Americans, music videos rank second only to friends as a trend source. The music genres of African-American origin—rap, R&B, hip hop, and dance, dominate airplay on many of teens' favorite radio and music-video stations. Teens, both black and white, look to music videos not only for the latest in music but also for the latest in fashion and language. Many of today's (and yesterday's) teen fashions originated with rappers.

A study of the hip-hop generation by a Philadelphia-based social sciences group reported that urban minority teens respect

# Where Teens Find Out About Trends

*Teens rate friends as the most important source for new trends.*

**(percent of teens citing source, 1994)**

|  | *percent* |
|---|---|
| Friends | 47% |
| Magazine | 32 |
| TV shows | 29 |
| Myself | 21 |
| Music videos | 19 |
| Advertising | 14 |
| "Coolest" people in school | 13 |
| DJ (radio) | 9 |
| Older brothers/sisters | 8 |
| Movies | 8 |
| Celebrities | 6 |
| "Weirdest" people in school | 4 |
| VJ (video) | 4 |
| Younger brothers/sisters | 3 |

Source: TRU *Teenage Marketing & Lifestyle Study*

rappers more than they do any other type of celebrity, including athletes. These teens believe rappers are more honest than other celebrities and that rappers portray their lives more accurately and relevantly than do athletes with multimillion dollar contracts. Given these perceptions, perhaps it's not surprising that significantly more African-American than white teens say they look to music videos for lifestyle cues.

About 20 percent of teens consider themselves to be trendsetters, saying they learn about trends from themselves. These are the teens who really feel great about themselves! Sixteen- and 17-year-old girls and 18- and 19-year-old boys rate themselves highest on this measure. We have found that fewer than 10 percent of teens are true trendsetters, however.

Do teens take cues from advertising, or do advertisers take cues from teens? This is a question marketers frequently ask. In fact, it works both ways. We know advertisers take cues from teens or there would be no need for teen research. Just as importantly, teens take cues from advertising. Fourteen percent name advertising as a prime source of trends. Because teens typically deny the influence of advertising, the 14 percent figure is undoubtedly understated. Nevertheless, teens admit that advertising is a more important trend source than DJs, VJs, movies, celebrities, or the coolest and weirdest people at school.

Again, if you want to know what's up with teens—or even more of a challenge, what's going to be up with teens next—pay attention to the same things teens do. Read what they read, watch what they watch, and go where they go. Nothing is more important than keeping your eyes and ears open!

## What's in, What's out

Adults view teens as extremely fickle, quickly adopting the latest fad or trend only to discard it just as fast. This perception is true, but only to a point. To be successful, you must separate the soon-to-die fads from the die-hard trends.

Our syndicated study asks teens what's "in" and what's "out." The results paint a timely, rich picture of teens today. The list includes a lot of "out" items, and every now and then a client challenges us by asking, "If you really knew what's 'in,' why are so many things you measure 'out'?" There are several answers to that question.

First, we measure some items that are "out" because many advertisers believe they are "in," such as torn jeans, certain words, classic rock, and so on. Second, we try diligently to identify emerging trends. We want to identify items that our clients can tie into before they become accepted by the main-stream. Finally, we're not perfect! Although we regularly con-duct focus groups to help us compile the list to be tested, qualitative research cannot substitute for quantitative. Though we may hear from 20 or 40 teens in a few markets that something is "in," our national sample may disagree.

To compile our list of items to be tested, we use three sources: 1) TRU's most recent syndicated study, to learn what's rising and should be included on the list or what's falling and should be dropped; 2) teens themselves, both in focus groups designed for this purpose and through regular and planned observation (in other words, we go where teens go—from malls to clubs to social events where we observe and talk with teens); 3) media sources, from MTV and The Box to 90210 and a long list of magazines.

When I first ordered a subscription to *Seventeen* years ago, I was one of only two TRU employees. Predictably, I received a form letter from the editor, congratulating me on becoming "an American girl in the know." Now, each of our staff members is assigned a variety of magazines to browse through, clip, and route each month. (I still get *Seventeen*.)

If you've ever guessed wrong in advertising to teens, you know that teens can be unforgiving. If they feel misrepresented or patronized, they often reject the advertised service or product. Knowing what's "in" and what's "out" can help you avoid some of the pitfalls in advertising and marketing to teens. Successfully differentiating between fads and trends can save you heartache and money. Trends are safe—and recommended—in teen marketing. Fads are inherently unstable and dangerous. Designer jeans are a trend, but Z Cavaricci was a fad. Rap is a trend, but Vanilla Ice was a fad.

The data on what teens view as "in" and "out" provide insights into executional elements in advertising and promotion, revealing "hot" product categories. To help marketers distinguish between fads and trends, we've classified more than 100 items TRU has been tracking over the past few years into three categories: "safe for marketing use," "unsafe for marketing use," "use at your own risk." Keep in mind that some of the items appearing on the "unsafe" list may be safe and highly appropriate if you're targeting a single gender or narrow age targets. For example, although we classify home video games as "unstable" among the total teen population, they are highly stable among boys. Similarly, although skateboarding is "out" among total teens, it's "in" among younger boys. And although miniskirts are "out" among girls, they're "in" among boys. (It's hard to believe we spent time and money figuring that one out, isn't it?)

# Teen Trends:
# Safe for Marketing Use

*Knowing what's "in" and what's "out" can
help you avoid some of the pitfalls in
advertising and marketing to teens.*

**(trends that are consistently "in" among all teens, 1992-94)**

Alternative music
Baggy clothes
Baseball caps
Black clothes
Caring about the environment
College clothing
College sports
Computers
Curly hair
Cut-offs
Dance music
Dating
Denim
Designer jeans
Eating healthy
Fast cars
Flannel shirts
Going to the beach
Going to the movies
Having a girlfriend/boyfriend
High-school sports
Hiking/camping
Homecomings
Hooded sweatshirts

Horoscopes
In-line skating
Long hair on girls
Long, baggy shorts
MTV Sports
Music videos
Partying
Pro sports
Pro-sports clothing
Proms
R&B
Rap
Renting videos
Sharing costs on a date
Shopping
Short hair on girls
(especially among girls!)
Short hair on guys
Straight hair
Studying
Taking photos
The word "cool"
The word "man"
Volunteering

Source: TRU *Teenage Marketing & Lifestyle Study*

# Teen Fads:
# Unsafe for Marketing Use

*Trends are safe, and recommended, in teen marketing.*
*Fads are inherently unstable and dangerous.*

**(items that have been consistently "out" among all teens, 1992-94)**

| | |
|---|---|
| 1960s things | Preppy fashions |
| 1970s things | Skateboarding |
| Babysitting | Snoopy |
| Being a vegetarian | Sonic the Hedgehog |
| Being patriotic | The military |
| Being politically correct | The phrase "411" |
| Bellbottoms | The phrase "livin' large" |
| Cigarettes | The word "babe" |
| Classic Rock | The word "bogus" |
| Comics | The word "chillin" |
| Dieting | The word "def" |
| Disco | The word "dope" |
| Drugs | The word "dude" |
| Eyeglasses | The word "foul" |
| "Funky" hair | The word "fresh" |
| Liquor | The word "funky" |
| Long hair on guys | The word "phat" |
| Looking "sloppy" | The word "righteous" |
| Lots of jewelry | The word "smooth" |
| Lots of makeup | The word "straight" |
| Pierced noses | The word "yo" |
| Ponytails | Tight clothes |

Source: TRU *Teenage Marketing & Lifestyle Study*

117

# Unstable Items:
# Use at Your Own Risk

*Some of the items on this list may be safe if you're targeting a single gender or narrow age targets.*

**(items that were "in" as of the fall 1994 study but have been unstable over the years; or items that have been measured for too short a period of time to predict their stability; or items that are just too close to call)**

Arcade videogames
Beavis & Butt-Head
Birthday parties
Bodysuits
Boxer shorts
Bra tops
Burgers
Caring about AIDS
Caring about politics
Cellular phones
Chokers
Coloring your hair
Country
Denim shirts
Doc Martens
Electronic pagers
Family dinners
Garfield
Getting dressed up
Getting into nature
Going to teen clubs
Grunge
Heavy Metal
High tops
Hiking boots
Hip hop
Home videogames
Jean jackets

Long nails
"Malling it"
Miniskirts
Minor-League sports apparel
Multiple pierced ears
No makeup
Pierced ears on boys
Pizza
Plaid clothing
Protesting
Pullover jackets
Reggae
Ren & Stimpy
Sandals
Stonewashed jeans
T-shirts with rock star logos
Tanning
Tattoos
The Simpsons
The word "sucks"
The word "sweet"
Tights/leggings
Top 40
Using mousse
Vests
Wearing pants low at the hips
Working out

Source: TRU *Teenage Marketing & Lifestyle Study*

## Teenagers' Social and Trend Hierarchy

Everyone knows there's a social pecking order among teens, particularly in high school. Teens cluster into groups that carry certain labels, such as jocks, nerds, stoners, ropers, granolas, preppies, geeks, headbangers, skaters, gangbangers, and wanna-be's. Each market, even each school, has its own names for teen groups or cliques. While the names might be different, the hierarchy is the same both across town and across the country.

Status and image drive teen hierarchy. The teens at the top are considered the "coolest," the ones other teens emulate or try to emulate. Below the top teens are the majority that form the mainstream, less-secure teens who strive to fit in by adopting the fashions and behaviors they think their peers will find "cool."

Then there are the teens who want to fit in but can't and accept this fact. Finally, there are teens who don't care about the teen social hierarchy, marching to the beat of a different drummer.

This hierarchy not only defines the lives of teenagers, it also can be applied to marketing objectives. Twelve years ago, TRU was the first company to segment teenagers by statistically grouping them into lifestyle or psychographic segments. (This analysis was initiated by the late motivation researcher Dr. Burleigh Gardner.) About four years ago, we concluded that our system was not as useful as it had been because the segments had begun to vary significantly by age. Because teens are already so highly segmented by age, a teen lifestyle segmentation system that contains an age bias would be useless. So we reinvented our system, which we call Teen/Types.

To create the new system, we first identified the variables that most segment teens by lifestyle and attitudes. These variables include basic values, self-perceptions, the meaning of "cool," revealing "in" and "out" items, taste in music (teens who are into alternative music are different from teens who are into rap), and jeans brand of choice (again, the teen who wears Wrangler is different from the teen who wears Girbaud).

We then statistically segmented teens using a hierarchical cluster analysis. This was performed by Dr. Abel Jeuland of the University of Chicago, our consultant in statistical analyses. The result is a segmentation system that matches marketing goals. Specifically, we were successful in identifying a teenage segment, albeit a small one, that other teens emulate.

We uncovered four major groups of teens: Influencers, Conformers, Passives, and Independents. Each of these groups is composed of several subsegments, although for marketing applications we prefer to look at just the four major typologies. While pigeonholing people into one of four groups is less than perfect, this segmentation system has proven to be a highly accurate and useful marketing tool.

While the four Teen/Types vary in size, the average age of each group is about 15. The variables that most strongly discriminate the Teen/Types are values, attitudes, lifestyle preferences, and activities, rather than age. This segmentation system reveals the attitudinal and lifestyle differences that set teens apart from one another, even within the same age group.

The hierarchy of the teen social world is revealed by the Teen/Types. New products, fashions, and activities are initiated by Influencers. They are adopted quickly by Conformers and more slowly by Passives. The Independents choose products, fashions, and activities based on individual interests and concerns, not by what's "in" or "out." Currently, Influencers are significantly more likely than other teens to say a variety of items are "in," including boxer shorts (92 percent), designer jeans (88

# The Four
# Teen Types

*TRU has uncoverd four major teenage typologies:*
*Influencers, Conformers, Passives, and Independents.*

**(teen types as a percent of teens and average age, 1994)**

|  | *percent* | *average age* |
|---|---|---|
| Conformers | 58% | 15.6 |
| Passives | 17 | 15.5 |
| Independents | 16 | 14.6 |
| Influencers | 9 | 15.6 |

Source: TRU *Teenage Marketing & Lifestyle Study*

percent), hiking boots (73 percent), going to teen clubs (68 percent), the word "smooth" (63 percent), surprisingly enough, preppy fashions (50 percent), and the word "straight" (48 percent). Because it is the nature of Influencers to influence, these items soon may become hot among mainstream teens as well.

## The Influencers

The top social group is also the smallest, comprising just 9 percent of the teen population. This is a highly select group. These are the teens most other teens "wanna be." For marketers, Influencers are the teens to reach first, because their actions are adopted by the majority.

Influencers are set apart from other teens by their outgoing nature and busy social life, and by their confidence in themselves and in their status among peers. These teens derive much of their confidence from the social status they already hold. They know they have "arrived," so to speak. They say "things are going extremely well" for them and that most people who know them (or even see them!) think they're "cool." Influencers simply enjoy being teen. They revel in this life stage and in the stature they have achieved.

Influencers are involved in the full range of social and athletic activities. They cite "hanging out with friends" as a primary activity, getting together with their friends an average of three or four nights a week. When out with friends, Influencers participate in a wide variety of activities, from partying to cruising and from shopping to volunteering. They get together with the opposite sex much more often than do other teens.

Influencer activities revolve around social events, from parties and concerts to movies, sports, eating out, and hanging out. Even school is a social event for these teens.

Influencers—both boys and girls—are active in a variety of sports. They are more likely than other teens to attend sporting events, consume sports media, be familiar with pro athletes, and to say that being on a school athletic team is "in."

To most teens, looking good is a key component of being "cool." So, Influencers not only have engaging personalities but also envied physical qualities. It is not surprising, then, that Influencers are more likely than other teens to cite good looks as a key ingredient to being "cool." Influencers work harder than other teens at maintaining their physical appearance. Male Influencers are more likely than other teen boys to read *GQ*. Female Influencers are avid readers of fashion magazines, including *Glamour*, *Cosmopolitan*, and *Vogue*. Influencers are also more likely than other teens to say being "popular with the opposite sex," "smart" and "independent" all contribute to being "cool."

Influencers love to spend time and money shopping. Female Influencers visit malls almost twice a week and frequent specialty apparel stores about once a week. Influencers shop at a wider variety of retail outlets than do other teens.

Influencers are experienced with money, earning and spending more money than other Teen/Types. Male Influencers are behind this difference, spending an average of $25 more a week than other teen boys and $18 more a week than Influencer girls. Influencers are more materialistic than other teens and more likely to agree with the statement: "Success means making a lot of money."

Influencers, more than other teens, say that good teen-directed advertising should be funny, shouldn't try too hard to be "cool," shouldn't preach, and should relate to teens. Yet

Influencers, more than other teens, say good advertising shouldn't try to be "teen," but it should be made for teens not parents. That's a fine line to walk. Because of their positive attitude toward advertising, Influencers are not only a key teen target, they are also the most receptive.

Although Influencers are self-confident, they still want to fit in with their peers. They've worked hard to attain their social status and they plan to maintain it. Consequently, they are particularly conscious of their physical appearance. These teens are more likely than others to own contact lenses. They buy more health care products such as acne remedies and antiperspirants/deodorants. Their spending on acne remedies is especially revealing, since they are least likely among the Teen/Types to suffer from acne. Evidently, prevention motivates these teens to buy acne medication. Influencer girls spend more money than other teens on hair care products, makeup, and jewelry. Influencers are more label conscious about clothes than are other teens.

Notably, this is the group that agrees most strongly with the statement, "I'm often the first one to try something new." Their urge to experiment is evident in their social activities and concerns. Influencers are more likely than other teens to enjoy in-line skating, for example. They are more likely to purchase expensive videogames, and they are more aware of the newest musical acts.

Not only do these teens play hard, they also have high expectations for their futures. They feel they will be successful in whatever they pursue. They plan to live better than their parents.

Fun scores well among Influencers, since fun is a major theme of their lives. Advertising and promotions that tie into socializing, music, and high-energy sports are especially appealing to these teens. Reaching these mobile, active teens where they play and work through radio, place-based media, key magazines, TV programs, and event marketing is likely to be effective.

## The Conformers

Conformers are the massive mainstream of teen life. They comprise the largest Teen/Type—nearly 60 percent of the teen population. They are typical teenagers, conforming to the latest teen styles and trends.

Conformers lack the self-confidence and social status of Influencers. Their insecurity makes them willing to adopt already-developed fads. Conformers are average participants in most activities. In fact, what most sticks out about this group is that nothing sticks out! They do not take extreme views or have deep-seated concerns. They are not the group most likely to buy any particular product. Their most noteworthy characteristic is that they effectively emulate Influencers.

The self-esteem of Conformers seems to be relatively low. Conformers are less likely than either Influencers or Independents to think they're "cool." They are least likely of all Teen/Types to think they're "normal," or that things are going well for them. They adopt ongoing styles and fads to boost their confidence in themselves and in how they wish others to see them. Conformers socialize, but to a lesser degree than Influencers. They are not as active as Influencers in social or athletic events, yet they participate in almost all the same things (parties, sports, and shopping). They get together with friends about three nights a week. They also talk on the phone with friends of both genders regularly.

Conformers have a wide variety of musical tastes (because they are trying to fit in) ranging from heavy metal and classic rock to top 40 and alternative. Rap, reggae, hip hop, and R&B are all more preferred by Influencers.

Conformers are trend followers rather than leaders. But significantly more Conformers than Passives say they are the first to try something new. Conformers agree with Influencers in their recommendations to advertisers. They also advise advertisers not to talk down to them, revealing their struggle for respect.

Conformers are more likely than Passives to say that being popular with the opposite sex, being smart, or being independent makes someone "cool." Conformers are more likely than Independents to say being funny, independent, a big partyer, rebellious, or having an outgoing personality makes people "cool."

Significantly more male than female Conformers agree that popularity with the opposite sex, athleticism, partying, and owning "cool" stuff makes someone "cool." More girls than boys say good looks, an outgoing personality, and how they dress makes someone "cool."

Conformers are mildly concerned about social issues, such as AIDS, child abuse, abortion, and drug abuse, but they are not activists in any of these areas.

Conformers are an important teen segment because they actively emulate Influencers, they have the financial means (i.e., high income and spending levels) to do so, and they represent the majority of the teen population. Because of its size and insecurity, this is the group from which marketers profit. Advertising and promotions that show what "cool" teens wear, do, or own can be especially effective with Conformers, giving them the cues they strive to adopt. Products or services that help solve typical teen problems and promote self-confidence are especially compelling to Conformers.

## The Passives

Like Conformers, Passives yearn to be popular and fit in with other teens. Yet they are notably more passive than Conformers in their attempt to emulate these teens. They are the least active teen group in general. They are the last to pick up on fashion trends. They spend less time listening to music than Influencers or Conformers. Fewer Passives than other Teen/Types say they try to have as much fun as possible. Passives exist on the margins of mainstream teen life, lacking the confidence and other personal attributes needed to elevate their status.

This Teen/Type is dominated by boys, with a three-to-one male to female ratio. This may explain why Passives are not stylistically "in," since boys are less fashion conscious than girls.

Just because Passives are less active than other teens does not mean they're completely unsociable. They have friends, typically other Passives, with whom they get together about three times a week. Even when they get together with their friends, though, they are less physically active than other teens. They are more likely than other teens to play board games, computer games, and use a computer at home and at school.

Notably, Passives seem more secure than Conformers. They are content with their place in the teenage social hierarchy, while Conformers hope to move up. Passives are more likely than Conformers to say "things are really going well" for them. Still, many Passives agree with the statement, "I wish I was more popular." They seem envious of their more popular peers and say it's important to "fit in" with the kids they like. While inwardly they may yearn to be like their "cool" peers, they aren't motivated enough or able to improve their situation. While acknowledging that they're not the "in" group, they believe they're part of a "normal" teen group. This feeling may contribute to their passive nature, since they feel securely surrounded by others like themselves.

Passives more than other Teen/Types think that being a good athlete makes someone "cool," possibly because of their lower level of athletic ability. Passives want to excel in athletics more than do Conformers or Independents. Passives are more likely than Independents to think someone their age who is funny, has an outgoing personality, or is rebellious is "cool." Finally, more Passives than Conformers say owning "cool" stuff makes people "cool." Not surprisingly, Passives don't like hip hop or dance music as much as other Teen/Types do. They're not socially active enough to be dance fans, nor cutting-edge enough to be hip hop fans.

Passives believe their lives as adults will be pretty much the same as those of their parents. They do not seem to care much about social issues, with the exception of AIDS and education.

While Passives spend less money than Influencers or Conformers, they're a worthwhile target, representing 20 percent of the teen population. While they are slower to adopt teen styles and fads than Conformers, they are still adopters and should respond favorably to the same messages that appeal to Conformers. Products and services that offer solutions to teen problems or that make Passives feel optimistic about their stage in life should be especially effective with this group.

## The Independents

Sixteen percent of the teen population falls into the Independent Teen/Type. Like Passives, Independents are outside the teen social circle looking in. They differ from Passives in that they are more confident about themselves, and they are content to remain on the outside. These are the teens who care the least about being "cool" and who profess the least interest in the teenage social hierarchy.

Independents are the least involved in typical teen social activities, such as hanging out with friends, going to parties, or getting together with the opposite sex. They spend an average of five nights a week at home alone without friends. Independents are not lacking for confidence. Quite the opposite is true: they believe things are going well for them and that they will be successful in the future.

Independents are more likely than other teens to take part in activities alone, such as watching TV or playing a musical instrument. They enjoy what they do, even if they do it on their own. Fewer Independents than other teens name "friends" when asked what sometimes stresses them out. Significantly more Independents than other teens say their religious faith is "one of the most important parts" of their lives and regularly attend religious functions.

Independents spend less time listening to FM radio or recorded music than other Teen/Types. This group also does not have a passion for any one style of music.

Independents care less about money than do other teens. They spend less than other teens, and they earn $24 a week less than the next poorest teen group.

Like other teens, Independents are concerned about AIDS and education, but this group is more concerned than Influencers or Conformers about violence in schools, drinking and driving, and drug abuse. This group is more politically involved than the other Teen/Types. Independents are more likely than other teens to say "being patriotic," "caring about politics," and "volunteering" are "in."

Consistent with their independent nature, there are no obvious patterns in the behavior of Independents. They pick and choose activities and interests that make them happy, conforming to their own desires rather than to those of the group. This segment is undoubtedly composed of several divergent subsegments, making Independents an unstable group.

Marketers should view Independents as a fringe group, albeit a significant one. They neither lead nor follow the trends. They buy products and services that appeal to their individual interests, concerns, and tastes. This makes them a difficult group to target, but they are also the least desirable target because of their low level of spending and their detachment from the teen social and consumer hierarchy. Interestingly, this group has more in common with Influencers than any other Teen/Type. While we do not recommend that you specifically target these teens, marketing campaigns directed at Influencers are likely to attract at least some Independents.

*Chapter Six*

*Teens and Music*

Music is probably the most influential and pervasive medium in teenage lives. It can reflect a teen's own personal experience, and it unites teens into a collective whole. But music not only reflects the teen experience, it also defines it. And it always has.

Because of music's power to attract and speak to teens, it is an effective marketing tool when used appropriately. From creating original rock jingles to signing on the biggest stars as endorsers, advertisers have used music to reach teens for more than 40 years. In the past 15 years or so, however, there has been an explosion in the number of companies and brands using music to communicate with teens.

In the early 1980s, Pepsi's use of Michael Jackson helped to define its image as distinct from Coke's. By effectively using someone who at the time was the hottest musical act among teens, Pepsi boosted its brand image. Teens perceived it as youthful, "cool," and relevant. Teens developed an ownership of Pepsi that remains today.

All teen marketers want to do the same for their brands, to make them relevant and compelling to teens. Music can help you do so. There are two ways to associate a brand with music or to use music in marketing or advertising to teens. One, tie into a specific act, like Pepsi did with Michael Jackson. Two, tie into a musical genre but not a specific artist. Each of these techniques has certain advantages.

Signing on with a current musical act can bring immediate attention to your brand, helping to create awareness. Unless your company is blessed with a huge budget and can move quickly into production, however, you probably will be better off using music without a celebrity. The greatest disadvantage of tying into a musical act is that its popularity is usually short-lived. More often than not, musical stars live or die on their latest product. Typically, it's only super brands like Pepsi or Coke that can afford to pay huge sums for short-term endorsement deals and quickly produce elaborate commercials that air during an act's short-lived ride at the top.

The key to using a musical celebrity is to select one who is on the way up but hasn't yet peaked. Because teens' musical taste is much more diversified than it once was, it's equally important to consider the genre in which the artist performs.

We use a measure called TRU*Scores to determine the relative popularity of celebrities. TRU*Scores show the percentage of teens familiar with an act who like the act "very much." Michael Jackson still holds the all-time highest TRU*Score for a musical act, a 60 he achieved in 1983 when *Thriller* was riding high on the charts. The score means that 60 percent of teens who were aware of Michael Jackson at the time liked him "very much."

The advantage of TRU*Scores are that they compare acts based on their popularity among those who are familiar with them, not on the size of their audience. The measure uncovers the less well-known acts that score well. Given greater exposure, these acts may become widely popular. Acts with a high TRU*Score—from the mid-30s on up—but with a low awareness quotient have potential as endorsers. Of course, this quantitative assessment is only your first step in choosing a celebrity. Matching an act's image to your corporate or brand image is the other determinant in deciding whether to pursue a deal.

Because of our experience in developing and working with TRU*Scores, we have become fairly skilled at predicting musical trends, particularly the rise and fall of certain acts. What follows are some rules we've developed about teen musical preferences.

# Highest TRU*Scores
# Among Musicians

*The key to using a musical celebrity is to select one
who is on the way up, but hasn't yet peaked.*

**(15 all-time highest TRU*Scores for musical acts; TRU*Scores are the
percentage of teens familiar with an act who like the act "very much")**

| TRU* Score | Performer | Wave |
|---|---|---|
| 60 | Michael Jackson | Spring 1984 |
| 57 | Madonna | Fall 1985 |
| 54 | Bon Jovi | Spring 1987 |
| 54 | M. C. Hammer | Fall 1990 |
| 53 | Men at Work | Fall 1983 |
| 53 | Journey | Spring 1984 |
| 53 | Whitney Houston | Fall 1986 |
| 53 | M. C. Hammer | Spring 1991 |
| 53 | Boyz II Men | Spring 1993 |
| 52 | Van Halen | Fall 1984 |
| 51 | Journey | Spring 1989 |
| 51 | Boyz II Men | Fall 1993 |
| 50 | Green Day | Spring 1995 |
| 50 | Boyz II Men | Spring 1992 |
| 50 | Bruce Springsteen | Fall 1985 |

Source: TRU *Teenage Marketing & Lifestyle Study*

These rules can guide you in deciding which type of music or which celebrity would work for your brand.

**Teens show an overwhelming preference for new music.** To a teen, "new" music doesn't mean "recent" or "within the last couple years." It means the newest music of all. Teens are attracted to new music because of a basic teen tenet: teens prefer things that are uniquely for them. This is true not only of music but of other lifestyle choices as well.

New musical acts can achieve fame with lightning speed. Because MTV connects teens globally, performers whose videos are in heavy rotation can gain a mass audience and teen fame almost overnight. Musical acts can lose their popularity just as rapidly. Because of teens' accelerated physiological and emotional growth, their preferences and tastes constantly change. One-fourth of the teen audience of a musical act that was "in" just two years ago will have aged out of the segment. The remaining three-fourths may associate the act with a time when they were "just kids."

Nothing can match the excitement of a debut. Another reason new acts can lose their appeal rapidly is that they cannot debut twice. Cyndi Lauper, Ace of Base, Men at Work, Tiffany, and New Kids on the Block are just a few examples of artists who debuted strongly with teens but lost their appeal as quickly as they gained fame. Because a debut is a singular occasion, artists (and their labels) must find other ways to match the excitement of newness after a debut.

One obvious way to do this is to create quality music; certainly this separates genuine talent from one-hit wonders. But even quality music may not be enough to maintain popularity among teens. Artists who innovate continuously are popular longer than those who do not innovate. Madonna has been one of the few artists who could reinvent herself enough to recapture a teen audience. Still, she has never come close to matching the popularity she enjoyed when she debuted.

**Commercial endorsements accelerate the erosion of an artist's popularity among teens.** As much as teens enjoy seeing one of their favorite music stars in a TV commercial, they often view commercial endorsements as "selling out." This exposure also means that an artist has gained acceptance by the mainstream. Performers who are also embraced by Mom and Dad or by younger brothers and sisters are often resoundingly rejected by teens. Teens prefer artists whom they can call their own.

Such was the case with Hammer. He debuted (as M. C. Hammer) to tremendous teen popularity and sustained it for a full year. Then he went commercial. Mattel introduced him in doll form as "Barbie's celebrity friend." He was featured in a Saturday-morning cartoon. He also sold Pepsi and British Knights (sneakers) in commercials. What happened was predictable: little kids (and some parents) started to love Hammer, but big kids wanted to pretend they never had.

Assuming that an artist's music and image are appealing, the common denominator in the popularity of musical acts among teens is newness. "Some music is only popular because it *is* new," one teen told me bluntly during a focus group.

An artist's popularity also can spiral downward from overexposure, triggered by endorsements, merchandise licensing, advertising, and publicity.

This creates a "Catch 22" situation when signing on a musical star. The star's effectiveness in communicating to teens will last only a short period of time, and the endorsement itself is likely to wear out the artist's popularity.

# Hammered:
# The Fast Rise and Fall
# of a Mainstream Rapper

*As much as teens enjoy seeing one of their favorite music stars in a TV commercial, they often view commercial endorsements as "selling out."*

**(M. C. Hammer's TRU\*Scores by study wave, fall 1990 to spring 1993; TRU\*Scores are the percentage of teens familiar with an act who like the act "very much")**

| Wave | TRU*Score |
|------|-----------|
| Fall 1990 | 54 |
| Spring 1991 | 53 |
| Fall 1991 | 40 |
| Spring 1992 | 31 |
| Fall 1992 | 25 |
| Spring 1993 | 20 |

Source: TRU *Teenage Marketing & Lifestyle Study*

Because of these problems, record labels are monitoring their artists' endorsement deals carefully. They understand that the short-term riches gained from commercial deals are often outweighed by the premature death of an artist's career. Of course, acts that are intrinsically faddish and destined to fade rapidly, such as Vanilla Ice or Milli Vanilli, will want to grab commercial endorsements while the getting is good.

**Musical acts have a one-year window of opportunity for gaining popularity among teens.** With the single exception of Boyz II Men, no act ever achieving a TRU*Score of at least 35 has been able to top that score in more than three waves (one-and-a-half years) of our syndicated study. This statistic alone shows how fickle teens are about musical performers.

Before Boyz II Men, Janet Jackson and Mariah Carey came close to breaking the "three-wave rule." But the popularity of both fell after two consecutive waves of TRU*Score increases. Both artists shied away from commercial endorsements and, like Boyz II Men, both are genuinely talented.

Acts with little talent can also rise to fame quickly, but they fall just as fast. Teens can't be fooled for long, though long enough for manufactured acts—propelled by gimmicks—to gain fame and fortune. To sustain any respectable level of popularity, an artist needs to be legitimate. Teens are discerning enough to reject acts that lack real talent. Hopefully, Vanilla Ice, New Kids on the Block, and Milli Vanilli put their money into long-term investments.

**Certain genres breed greater teen loyalty.** Most musical acts have an extremely short shelflife among teens. Top-scoring artists (with TRU*Scores over 40) begin to decline in popularity after a maximum of one year. But even with lower scores, acts can

# Acts With Fleeting Popularity

*Most musical acts have an extremely*
*short shelflife among teens.*

**(highest and lowest TRU\*Scores for listed artists as of fall 1993;**
**TRU\*Scores are the percentage of teens familiar with**
**an act who like the act "very much")**

|  | *highest* | *lowest* |
|---|---|---|
| Michael Jackson | 60 | 6 |
| Madonna | 57 | 18 |
| Bruce Springsteen | 50 | 8 |
| Vanilla Ice | 45 | 8 |
| New Kids on the Block | 45 | 5 |

# Acts With Loyal Fans

*Even with lower scores, acts can develop*
*loyal fans among teens.*

**(highest and lowest TRU\*Scores for listed artists as of fall 1993)**

|  | *highest* | *lowest* |
|---|---|---|
| Boyz II Men | 53 | 45 |
| Mariah Carey | 41 | 31 |
| Guns 'N Roses | 30 | 29 |
| Pearl Jam | 37 | 31 |

Source: TRU *Teenage Marketing & Lifestyle Study*

develop loyal fans among teens. Teen loyalty depends somewhat on the musical genre, with some genres developing more loyal fans than others.

The success of Boyz II Men, like that of Mariah Carey, is explained by their appeal to all teen segments. As teens' musical tastes have become more fragmented, Boyz II Men's vocal talents and non-alienating image helped them win unprecedented popularity among the entire teen population.

Overall, alternative and hard rock groups generate greater loyalty among teens. Pearl Jam, Nirvana, the Red Hot Chili Peppers, Metallica, and Guns 'N Roses may never be as popular among all teens as some of the R&B and top-40 stars, such as Boyz II Men, Janet Jackson, or Mariah Carey. But their fans are more loyal, and, therefore, their TRU*Scores are more stable. Guns 'N Roses' popularity among teens has become predictable, scoring a 29 or 30 in the last five consecutive waves of our study. (What the members of this band do offstage is less predictable. Not many companies want their brands associated with Axyl, Slash, and the gang.)

TRU*Scores are important for advertisers because they measure the popularity of performers among all teens, not just record-buying teens. It's important to recognize that while most teens buy music, a significant minority do not. According to our syndicated study, nearly 30 percent of teens did not buy a CD or prerecorded tape in the past year. With few exceptions, most advertisers want to reach the masses. One exception would be a record-buying club, which would want to target music-buying teens.

Teens who buy music regularly have different musical tastes than those who don't. Heavy music buyers have a harder edge to their musical taste. They are more likely to prefer rap,

# Heavy Buyers vs. Non Buyers: Musical Genre Preferences

*Teens who buy music regularly have different musical tastes than those who don't.*

**(percent saying genre is "in"; heavy buyers are those who have shopped at a record store more than five times in the past 30 days; nonbuyers have not shopped in a record store in the past 30 days; 1993)**

|  | percent | |
|---|---|---|
|  | **heavy buyers** | **non-buyers** |
| **Preferred significantly more by heavy buyers:** | | |
| Rap | 81% | 73% |
| Hip Hop | 71 | 56 |
| R&B | 67 | 53 |
| Reggae | 62 | 44 |
| Alternative | 61 | 46 |
| Heavy Metal | 61 | 53 |
| **Preferred significantly more by non buyers:** | | |
| Country | 41 | 51 |
| **Preferred equally by both heavy and non buyers:** | | |
| Classic Rock | 45 | 48 |
| Top 40 | 61 | 57 |

Source: TRU *Teenage Marketing & Lifestyle Study*

# Heavy Buyers vs. Non Buyers: Musical Performer Preferences

*Today, African-American teens determine the
musical preferences of the teen majority,
with black genres now the favorites of teens.*

(TRU*Scores for musical acts; heavy buyers are those who have shopped
at a record store more than five times in the past 30 days; nonbuyers have
not shopped in a record store in the past 30 days, fall 1993; TRU*Scores are
the percentage of teens familiar with an act who like the act "very much")

|  | TRU*Scores | |
|---|---|---|
|  | *heavy buyers* | *non-buyers* |
| **Preferred significantly more** | | |
| **by heavy buyers:** | | |
| Dr. Dre | 53 | 48 |
| Pearl Jam | 45 | 27 |
| Metallica | 35 | 24 |
| REM | 32 | 23 |
| Alice in Chains | 27 | 14 |
| **Preferred significantly more** | | |
| **by non buyers:** | | |
| Boyz II Men | 48 | 54 |
| Fresh Prince | 34 | 38 |
| **Preferred by both** | | |
| **heavy and non buyers:** | | |
| Shai | 49 | 48 |
| Whitney Houston | 42 | 41 |
| Michael Jackson | 24 | 22 |

Source: TRU *Teenage Marketing & Lifestyle Study*

heavy metal, and alternative. They also prefer hip hop, reggae, and R&B more than nonbuyers do. Those who don't buy much music like country more than heavy-buying teens do. They like top-40 and classic rock about as much as heavy buyers do. The preceding tables compare the musical preferences of heavy buyers (those who have shopped at a record store more than five times in the past 30 days) with teens who haven't shopped at a record store in the past 30 days.

**African-American genres are the most popular among teens.** What's popular among African-American teens influences the white majority. This is true not only in music, but also in fashion and language. Not long ago, the musical preferences of white teens determined an artist's popularity among all teens. Today, African-American teens determine the musical preferences of the teen majority, with essentially black genres—rap, hip hop, dance, and R&B—now the favorites of teens, although alternative is gaining quickly.

The popularity of these genres is particularly noteworthy since black performers were, to some degree, barred from mainstream commercial exposure as late as the 1980s. The unprecedented success of Michael Jackson's *Thriller* and the acceptance of his videos on MTV broke through this racial barrier. Today it is not uncommon for white artists to achieve popularity by working in a black genre.

The following table shows the growing influence of African-American performers. It lists the top-scoring artist in each of TRU's past 22 waves, with black performers denoted in boldfaced type. Beginning around 1990, African-American artists became the most popular musical acts among all teens. Notice that in 1995, for the first time in four years (eight studies), a white act (Green Day) was number one.

# Top Musical Acts, 1984 to 1995

*Beginning around 1990, African-American artists became the most popular musical acts among all teens.*

**(most popular musical acts in past 20 waves of *Teenage Marketing & Lifestyle Study*; black performers in bold)**

| *Wave* | *Performer* |
|--------|-------------|
| Spring 1995 | Green Day |
| Fall 1994 | **R. Kelly** |
| Spring 1994 | **Snoop Doggy Dogg** |
| Fall 1993 | **Boyz II Men** |
| Spring 1993 | **Boyz II Men** |
| Fall 1992 | **Kris Kross** |
| Spring 1992 | **Boyz II Men** |
| Fall 1991 | **Bell Biv DeVoe** |
| Spring 1991 | **M. C. Hammer** |
| Fall 1990 | **M. C. Hammer** |
| Spring 1990 | Paula Abdul |
| Fall 1989 | New Kids on the Block |
| Spring 1989 | George Michael |
| Fall 1988 | George Michael |
| Spring 1988 | **Whitney Houston** |
| Fall 1987 | Lisa/Cult Jam |
| Spring 1987 | Bon Jovi |
| Fall 1986 | Bon Jovi |
| Spring 1986 | Bruce Springsteen |
| Fall 1985 | Madonna |
| Spring 1985 | Van Halen |
| Fall 1984 | Journey |
| Spring 1984 | **Prince** |

Source: TRU *Teenage Marketing & Lifestyle Study*

**Rap is here to stay because it speaks more powerfully to teens than any other genre.** It has been said that rap is the first recent major cultural phenomenon that did not come from baby boomers. This is one reason for its popularity among teens. They own rap; it speaks directly to them. Rap also appeals to teens because, like dance and R&B, it's a rhythmic genre.

Over the past few years, rap has evolved considerably, as evidenced by the differing styles of M. C. Hammer and Dr. Dre. Today, there are "mainstream" rappers, gangsta rappers, female rappers, jazz rappers, and other hybrid rap performers.

**Although teens favor rap, they still love great singers.** Although rap is the most popular genre, the most popular performers among teens are those who combine good vocals and a strong R&B rhythm. In what may be a backlash against the proliferation of nonmelodic rap, there are a growing number of great vocal R&B groups, such as Boyz II Men, Shai, Silk, and En Vogue. Teens are also enthusiastic about solo artists whom they judge to be talented vocalists, such as Mariah Carey, Whitney Houston, and Mary J. Blige.

**Classic rock and country are less relevant to teens.** Though some teens tell me they "respect" the great rock-and-roll artists, such as the Beatles, the Stones, Led Zeppelin, or the Grateful Dead, they recognize that this music belongs to another generation (namely, their parents'). In each wave of our syndicated study, we measure the popularity of one or two classic rockers. Predictably, their scores are low. The Beatles fared poorly among teens even at the time their catalog was released on CD and received a great deal of media attention. Eric Clapton received a low score even when his album, *Unplugged*, was riding high on the charts and his performance on MTV was shown repeatedly.

# Most Popular Musical Genres Among Teens

*Rap is here to stay because it speaks more powerfully to teens than any other genre.*

**(percent of teens saying genre is "in," 1995)**

|  | *percent* |
|---|---|
| Rap/gangsta rap/hip hop (net) | 75% |
| Alternative | 68 |
| Dance | 63 |
| R&B | 58 |
| Top 40 | 58 |
| Heavy Metal | 57 |
| Reggae | 52 |
| Classic Rock | 48 |
| Country | 47 |
| Disco | 17 |

Source: TRU *Teenage Marketing & Lifestyle Study*

The only exception to the poor performance of classic rockers is Queen's TRU*Score of 32, received when the movie *Wayne's World* was showing in theaters. Wayne, Garth, and their buddies lip-synching to the Queen classic "Bohemian Rhapsody" (which became a heavily rotated MTV video) was perhaps teens' favorite scene in this blockbuster movie. Clearly, it takes a lot before a classic rock act scores well among teens.

Country music has been one of the fastest-growing genres among adults and teens over the past few years. Still, country is limited to more of a cult following among teens, and it is rejected by teens in the Northeast. Teens do not feel that they "own" country, nor is it particularly relevant to their lives. Country has produced only a few artists (Garth Brooks, Tim McGraw, and John Michael Montgomery) whom teens respect. And unlike dance or rock, country does not offer the rhythm that so engages teens.

*Chapter Seven*

*Choosing the Right Celebrity*

Celebrities are an integral part of youth culture. To teens, they are more than musicians, athletes, actors, or fashion models. They are role models, heroes, and even icons. They do more than entertain teens. They nationalize the teen experience, speaking for a generation and inspiring trends in lifestyles, fashions, attitudes, and behavior. Celebrities can bring attention, authority, and added appeal to your teen-directed advertising and promotions.

Celebrities are human beings, however, and can be a risk if you wish to leverage their fame. Though not an endorser of a teen brand, O. J. Simpson is the most dramatic example of the risk you take when you tie into a celebrity. Michael Jackson and Tonya Harding (both of whom endorsed major teen brands) are other examples of celebrities who, because of allegations of wrongdoing, have become damaged goods to companies looking for endorsers.

Though teens have become more cynical about celebrities because so many have disappointed them, the right celebrity can still bring instant attention and credibility to your product or brand. I was reminded of this when we were testing a Nintendo TV spot for the company's "Ken Griffey, Jr. Presents Major League Baseball" game for the Super Nintendo Entertainment System. (Ken Griffey, Jr. is teen boys' second-favorite baseball player, behind Frank Thomas.) The primary objective of the research was to learn whether the execution clearly communicated its intended messages. But we heard something else of great importance during the research. As soon as the boys discovered that Ken Griffey, Jr. had lent his name to the game, their expectations of the game increased greatly. In this case, just the use of a celebrity's name heightened the image of the product. The right athlete can be a powerful marketing tool.

There are many other examples of the successful use of celebrities in marketing, none bigger than Michael Jordan. Jordan is teens' all-time favorite celebrity. He is vitally important to Nike's bottom line; the "Air Jordan" shoe line alone represents a substantial portion of Nike's basketball shoe sales. Being associated with Michael Jordan has also benefited Gatorade, McDonalds, Coca-Cola (before Gatorade), Wheaties, Wilson, Hanes, and other brands and licensees.

Maybe there will never be another Michael Jordan. But there are plenty of other exciting celebrities with whom you can associate. Shaquille O'Neal and Grant Hill appear to be Michael's heirs-apparent in basketball marketing, but an athlete from another sport or a celebrity from another field may emerge as the next teen super hero.

If you want to tie into celebrities, music and sports are the first two places to look. After music, sports is the area of interest shared by the largest number of teens. When we asked teens in our quantitative study which types of celebrities they most like to see in advertising, the winners by far were music and sports stars. Significantly more boys than girls chose sports stars, while significantly more girls than boys chose music stars.

After athletes and musicians come super models, a category that is relatively new. When we ask girls what they think about these glamorous models they frequently tell us, "I just can't relate to THAT!" Super models are beyond a typical teen girl's aspirational set. Consequently, twice as many boys as girls named super models as the celebrities they want to see in advertising.

During qualitative research we conducted, however, high-school boys were not enthusiastic when shown a brochure featuring a super model on its cover. One boy finally explained that he would prefer to see someone on the cover whom he would "actually have a shot at, like one of the best-looking girls at school" over the glamorous, older model. It appears that super models are also outside boys' aspirational set!

After super models, teens name movie stars, animated characters, and TV stars as the type of celebrity they most like to see in advertising. Note that teens' top three choices—sports stars, music stars, and models—are real people, rather than actors or characters in roles. Teens want honesty and clarity in advertising (almost above all else), so it follows that they want real-life endorsers rather than actors.

In addition to musical performers, we also track the popularity of sports and other stars with our TRU*Score system. By comparing the TRU*Score trends of celebrities in different fields, we have developed the following guidelines to help you determine which type of celebrity to sign up.

**Sports stars and certain actors and models are more popular than music stars.** Over the past three waves of our syndicated study, sports stars have averaged a TRU*Score of 41, compared to a 36 (one wave only) for actors/models and 28 for music stars. But it's important to remember that while sports stars win the popularity contest, a larger share of teens are familiar with actors/models and musical artists. On average, 76 percent of teens are familiar with music stars, and 68 percent are familiar with actors/models. But only 56 percent of teens, on average, are familiar with athletes. Fewer teens are familiar with sports stars simply because many girls don't know who these athletes are.

**The popularity of sports stars is more stable than that of musical acts, while the popularity of actors/athletes may be more stable than that of sports stars.** Musical acts typically

# Celebrity Types Teens Prefer in Advertising

*Sports and music stars are the types of celebrities teens most like to see in advertising.*

**(percent of teens preferring celebrity type in advertising, by gender, 1993)**

|  | *boys* | *girls* |
|---|---|---|
| Sports stars | 42% | 16% |
| Music stars | 12 | 33 |
| Super models | 22 | 12 |
| Movie stars | 8 | 16 |
| Animated characters | 11 | 11 |
| TV stars | 4 | 12 |

Source: TRU *Teenage Marketing & Lifestyle Study*

enjoy an extremely short span of popularity because teens like music that is new. The popularity of athletes lasts longer than that of musicians because each sport season brings them renewed attention. Eventually, however, age or physical problems end athletic careers and the popularity of sports stars among teens. Unlike athletes or musicians, actors can rejuvenate a waning career by starring in a new, successful TV show or movie. This can make the popularity of actors/models more stable than that of musicians or athletes.

**The appeal of sports stars, actors, and models is broader than that of musical performers.** Some of the sports starts, actors, and models admired by teens are also admired by their parents. Teens and parents are equally likely to be fans of Michael Jordan or Bill Cosby, for example. But in general, teen celebrity preferences are distinct from those of adults, as revealed in a comparison of celebrity preferences reported in our teen studies with a 1993 survey by Video Storyboard Tests. Candice Bergen was the most popular celebrity among adults at the time but ranked 32 out of 39 among teens. Cher was third most-popular among adults but next to last among teens.

**Certain musical acts appeal specifically to teens.** From thrash metal to gangsta rap, complete genres of music alienate adults. And teens love this. It gives them an important sense of ownership. The fact that adults don't like certain types of music is attractive to teens, since they want things that are uniquely their own. While adults might wear many of the same fashions as teens or get involved in the same activities, it's the rare parent who cranks up White Zombies or dances to Dr. Dre.

**Commercial endorsements increase the popularity of sports stars but erode the popularity of musical celebrities.**

Teens want music performers to remain pure. They see them as artists and can reject them for selling out if they endorse a commercial product. On the other hand, commercial endorsements can actually increase the popularity of athletes. Teens like Larry Johnson as much for his appealing "Grandmama" commercials for Converse as they do for being an all-star forward for the Charlotte Hornets. Charles Barkley, Bo Jackson, Deion Sanders, Tim Hardaway, Chris Webber, Emmitt Smith, Alonzo Mourning, and Dennis Rodman, to name just a few, are athletes whose starring roles in athletic-shoe commercials have broadened and heightened their teen appeal.

How can you narrow the field of celebrities who could endorse your brands? Select a celebrity who is on the way up, rather than someone who is at the peak of popularity. This is because teens are most attracted to what or who is new and because the budgets for many teen brands are relatively small. To find rising stars, we look for celebrities with a low familiarity ranking (meaning few teens are familiar with him or her) and a high popularity ranking (among the few teens who are familiar with the celebrity, he or she is highly popular). For example, Jerry Rice ranks 19th in familiarity among teens, but among those familiar with him, he ranks second in popularity.

During the time this study was fielded, these celebrities showed special potential as endorsers. All enjoyed a high degree of popularity among the relatively few teens who were familiar with them. If a celebrity is highly popular among the small audience familiar with him or her, then greater exposure should offer great promise.

The gap between a celebrity's familiarity and popularity is only the first screening step in deciding whom to sign on as an

# Celebrities With Endorsement Potential

*Select a celebrity who is on the way up, rather than someone who is at the peak of popularity.*

(familiarity ranking is based on the percent of teens who say they are familiar with a celebrity; popularity ranking is based on the percent of teens familiar with a celebrity who really like the celebrity; 1995; 1 is highest rank)

|  | familiarity ranking | popularity ranking |
|---|---|---|
| **Sports Stars** | | |
| Jerry Rice | 19 | 2 |
| Shawn Kemp | 20 | 4 |
| Steve Young | 21 | 10 |
| Frank Thomas | 27 | 9 |
| **Music Stars** | | |
| Stone Temple Pilots | 14 | 5 |
| Green Day | 17 | 1 |
| R Kelly | 23 | 6 |
| Offspring | 25 | 3 |
| Da Brat | 26 | 7 |
| **Actors and Models** | | |
| Damon Wayans | 20 | 3 |
| Dana Carvey | 23 | 4 |
| Keanu Reeves | 26 | 9 |
| Mark-Paul Gosselaar | 31 | 10 |
| Andrew Shue | 32 | 11 |

Source: TRU *Teenage Marketing & Lifestyle Study*

endorser. The next step is to examine the image and personality of the celebrity to assess whether there is a fit with your product, brand, and company. A gangsta rapper, for example, would be a bad bet, regardless of how popular he is.

## Using Sports Celebrities as Endorsers

While rap and alternative are teen's top musical preferences, basketball is king in sports. In the past several waves of our study, the highest sports TRU*Scores have belonged to basketball players, and to Michael Jordan in particular. In a recent wave, for example, basketball player Shawn Kemp, who was not a Dream Team I member (at that time there was no such thing as Dream Team II) or All-Star starter, scored significantly higher than hockey legends Wayne Gretsky and Mario Lemieux, baseball superstar Ken Griffey, Jr., or then pro-football MVP, Steve Young.

It's no coincidence that basketball players are the pro-athletes used most often advertising, not only for athletic shoes but also for fast-food and soft drinks. Teens like to see sports stars in commercials. This does not mean that teens do not discriminate, even among basketball players. They favor players who are the most exciting and physically gifted, including Michael Jordan, Shaquille O'Neal, Scottie Pippen, and Shawn Kemp. Behind the popularity of basketball players is the tremendous job the NBA has done in marketing itself and the sport. The NFL, the NHL, and major league baseball lag behind. Individual sports, such as tennis, track & field, boxing, ice skating, and auto racing, have been unable to produce the types of stars teens can relate to.

Some football stars are starting to move up, especially among boys. (Football stars historically receive higher scores in our spring studies, which are fielded during football season.) All-star running backs Emmitt Smith and Barry Sanders along with

# TRU*Scores for Athletes

*Nineteen of the top 20 highest scores to date belong to basketball players.*

**(all-time highest TRU*Scores for athletes, study waves, fall 1992-spring 1995; TRU*Scores are the percentage of teens familiar with an athlete who like the athlete "very much")**

| TRU*Score | athlete | wave |
|---|---|---|
| 66 | Michael Jordan | Fall 1992 |
| 64 | Michael Jordan | Spring 1992 |
| 63 | Michael Jordan | Fall 1993 |
| 62 | Michael Jordan | Spring 1993 |
| 62 | Shaquille O'Neal | Fall 1993 |
| 61 | Michael Jordan | Spring 1994 |
| 60 | Shaquille O'Neal | Spring 1994 |
| 60 | David Robinson | Fall 1992 |
| 59 | Scottie Pippen | Fall 1992 |
| 58 | Emmitt Smith | Spring 1994 |
| 57 | Michael Jordan | Fall 1994 |
| 57 | Magic Johnson | Spring 1992 |
| 56 | Michael Jordan | Spring 1995 |

Source: TRU *Teenage Marketing & Lifestyle Study*

*(continued)*

*(continued from previous page)*

| TRU*Score | athlete | wave |
|-----------|---------|------|
| 56 | Magic Johnson | Fall 1992 |
| 56 | Shaquille O'Neal | Fall 1994 |
| 56 | Scottie Pippen | Spring 1994 |
| 54 | Magic Johnson | Spring 1993 |
| 54 | Shaquille O'Neal | Fall 1992 |
| 54 | Shaquille O'Neal | Spring 1993 |
| 54 | Scottie Pippen | Spring 1992 |
| 54 | Scottie Pippen | Spring 1993 |
| 53 | Bo Jackson | Spring 1992 |
| 53 | Jerry Rice | Spring 1995 |
| 52 | David Robinson | Fall 1993 |
| 52 | Shawn Kemp | Fall 1993 |
| 52 | Magic Johnson | Fall 1993 |
| 52 | Jerry Rice | Spring 1994 |
| 51 | Emmitt Smith | Fall 1993 |
| 51 | Emmitt Smith | Spring 1995 |
| 51 | David Robinson | Spring 1992 |
| 51 | Kristi Yamaguchi | Fall 1992 |

Source: TRU *Teenage Marketing & Lifestyle Study*

legendary receiver Jerry Rice and media icon Deion Sanders have current scores among boys that are surpassed only by Michael Jordan's. As the table shows, 19 of the top 20 and 24 of the 31 highest scores to date belong to basketball players. Only one female athlete makes this list.

## Using Actors and Models as Endorsers

We have measured nonmusic, nonsport celebrities in only one wave of our syndicated study so far. But in that one analysis, we've detected preliminary patterns that can help you assess the popularity of actors and models.

Four of the five most-popular actors have roots in comedy, emphasizing the importance of using humor to attract teens. Teens' favorite TV shows are situation comedies, and their favorite commercials are those that use humor.

Five of the top-rated celebrities are stars of current TV shows, reflecting the impact of network TV in the lives of teens. Will Smith, the star of "The Fresh Prince of Bel-Air," received the highest TRU*Score of any celebrity. His score of 63 has been topped in earlier waves only by living-legend Michael Jordan. Teens are also familiar with Will Smith in his role as half of the rap duo DJ Jazzy Jeff and the Fresh Prince. Acting in "Fresh Prince" adds to his appeal. Now that he has co-starred in three major motion pictures, he's become a multimedia star.

A final note: actors and comedians have an inherent advantage over musicians and athletes in advertising. They can truly act.

*Chapter Eight*

*Teen Values*

$T$o communicate with teens effectively, you need to understand them on many levels. You need to understand what teens look like, how they act, what they think, and how they feel. You need to understand teen preferences and priorities. You need to know how teens see themselves and those close to them. You need to know the fundamental motivations that drive teen behavior: teen attitudes and values.

For several years, TRU has been tracking teen attitudes by asking teens whether they agree or disagree with more than 20 value statements. The results show trends in teen values over time. Attitudes change more slowly than behavior, even among teens. When attitudes do change, teen behavior is also likely to change since attitudes influence behavior.

We call the series of attitude statements we track the Teen Value Monitor. The Value Monitor reveals the teen mindset and "heartset." Its results can guide you in communicating effectively with teens.

## A Sense of Belonging and Acceptance

Many adults view teens as rebellious and nonconforming. If you hold this opinion, you may feel at a loss for how to appeal to this group. TRU's research destroys this teen stereotype, revealing how much teens want to be accepted by others. A greater proportion of teens say they like being with their family, for example, than say they wish to be more popular. Two-thirds of teens say they prefer having a couple of close friends to having many acquaintances.

Teens strive to fit in. The need to fit in and be accepted is a constant of this life stage and perhaps the most important motivator of teen behavior. About three out of five teens consider themselves "like most other kids," and a slightly smaller percent-

# Teens Want to Belong

*The need to belong to a close-knit group is more
important to older teens. Younger teens, in contrast,
yearn for widespread acceptance.*

**(percent of teens who agree strongly/somewhat
with each statement, by age, 1994)**

| | total | 12-15 | 16-17 | 18-19 |
|---|---|---|---|---|
| It's more important to have one or two close friends than many acquaintances. | 67% | 63% | 69% | 75% |
| I really like to do things with my family. | 63 | 66 | 60 | 62 |
| I think I'm pretty "normal"—most kids I know are pretty much like me. | 63 | 67 | 60 | 59 |
| I care a lot about whether my clothes are "in style." | 61 | 68 | 58 | 48 |
| It's important to me to "fit in" with my friends and other kids I like, and—to be real honest—sometimes their opinions can really influence me. | 48 | 59 | 40 | 33 |
| I wish I was more popular. I watch the kids who are popular and wish I was more like them. | 27 | 34 | 23 | 16 |

Source: TRU *Teenage Marketing & Lifestyle Study*

age care a lot about whether their clothes are "in style." Nearly half find it so important to fit in that they admit to being influenced by peer pressure.

There are significant differences in these belonging/acceptance measures among the age groups. The need to belong to a close-knit group is more important to older teens. Younger teens, in contrast, yearn for widespread acceptance. As adolescents age, their confidence and sense of self grow. With this growth comes a diminished need to be accepted by everyone and a greater desire to develop stronger bonds with fewer people.

One of the attitudes we track measures the importance of peer pressure: "It's important to me to fit in with my friends and other kids I like, and, to be real honest, sometimes their opinions can really influence me." As expected, the youngest teens are most willing to admit that they are influenced by peers. Teens aged 12 to 15 give more credence than older teens do to the opinions of others. Consequently, their self-image is largely dependent upon how they feel others see them. As teens age, they become less concerned about being popular, fitting in, and wearing what everybody else wears. They begin to develop a stronger sense of self and confidence in their unique attributes, feelings, and opinions. Nevertheless, a substantial minority of 18- and 19-year-olds also admit to being influenced by peer pressure, showing how powerful peer pressure can be.

"I had to cut my hair and dress like other people just to fit in," one 13-year-old girl told us in a focus group. "There's a lot of pressure to not be yourself."

Another teen girl, aged 14, told us, "The biggest thing is looking thin. All the models in magazines are extremely thin, and they look good. People in my school think that if you're not thin, you're not in."

A 13-year-old boy said, "In order to fit in, I'll have to wear the right clothes and lose some weight."

There are few differences in these belonging/acceptance attitudes by gender. Reflecting the greater family orientation of girls, more older girls (18 to 19) than older boys like to do things with their families (68 percent vs. 55 percent). Boys aged 16 or older are slightly more peer influenced than girls (39 percent vs. 34 percent).

We also track a less direct peer pressure statement: "I care a lot about whether my clothes are in style." Not only does this statement indicate how fashion conscious teens are, it is also a measure of independent thinking vs. group pressure. The operative phrase in the statement is "in style," meaning accepted by peers. As with the more direct statement about peer pressure, the youngest teens are most likely to agree with the statement, while the oldest are least likely.

The statement, "I think I'm pretty normal—most kids I know are pretty much like me," is designed to reveal how comfortable teens are with their view of themselves. If teens do not feel normal, they probably feel insecure and lonely.

When TRU does concept testing in focus groups, we often start out by asking teens to list the names of the social groups in their school. We hear many of the old standards: nerds, jocks, and preps. We also hear labels that are indigenous to certain regions: ropers in Texas, surfers in California, granolas in the Northwest. Of course, there are also gang and ethnic-related labels, such as taggers, gangbangers, wacks, wiggers (white kids who wish they were black), and R.I.C.s (racial identity crisis). After we expose the group to the concepts we want to discuss, we return to the labels and ask, "OK, which of these groups would like (buy, wear, try, etc.) this new idea?" If the answer is "nerds" or "geeks," there probably is a big problem with the concept. If the more popular types are the ones perceived to buy into the idea, then the concept has withstood the all-important test of the teen social hierarchy.

Sometimes, for our own curiosity, we ask, "Which of these groups do you fit into?" More often than not, teens will tell us, "I don't fit into any of these. I'm just normal!" Teens who feel normal are close enough to the teen mainstream to feel they belong and are accepted. Certainly, the boundaries of normalcy have expanded in teens' minds over the past several years. But, being part of the norm is a safe and desirable place to be for most teens. Those who don't feel normal fit into one of two camps: 1) those who are uncomfortably outside the teenage social mainstream; or 2) the more fortunate ones who think they're too cool to be classified as normal.

We've tracked changes in the belonging/acceptance measures over the past few years. Teens place more emphasis on having a few good friends rather than many acquaintances in 1993 than they did in 1991. They are less influenced by peer pressure, shown in the decline in the percent agreeing with having clothes that are in style, wanting to be more popular, and feeling that it's important to fit in. This would suggest that teens today are more mature than those just a few years ago. They recognize the importance of having a few people who are close to them. Yet they continue to struggle with the transition from child to adult.

## Striving for Identity

One of the challenges in marketing to teens is that this age group is marked by contradictory attitudes. Perhaps the most obvious contradiction is that as important as it is for teens to belong to a

# Changes in Belonging/Acceptance Values

*Teens placed more emphasis on having a few good friends rather than many acquaintances in 1993 than they did in 1991.*

**(percent of teens agreeing strongly/somewhat with each statement, 1991-1993)**

|  | *1993* | *1992* | *1991* |
|---|---|---|---|
| Important to have one or two close friends | 67% | 60% | 59% |
| Like to do things with my family | 63 | 69 | 68 |
| I care if my clothes are in style | 61 | 67 | 70 |
| Important to fit in/influenced by others | 48 | 52 | 51 |
| I wish I was more popular | 27 | 31 | 32 |

Source: TRU *Teenage Marketing & Lifestyle Study*

group and be accepted by others, it's equally important for them to carve out their own unique identity. Respondents will tell us in the same breath, "Hey, I want to fit in, but I don't want to be like everybody else!" These opposing psychological needs drive many teen behaviors.

Although teen responses to our belonging/acceptance measures seem mature and perhaps uncharacteristic of teens, their responses to the stereotypically teen statement, "I always try to have as much fun as I possibly can—I don't know what the future holds and I don't care what others think," are very teenlike. Nearly 70 percent strongly or somewhat agree with this statement. This is a timeless, engaging teen perspective. This attitude uniquely appeals to and is characteristic of this life stage: embracing the moment with a disregard for consequences. It is perhaps the quintessential teen statement. In fact, this message has been at the heart of several teen-directed campaigns, such as Pepsi's compelling, "Be Young. Have Fun. Drink Pepsi."

"The greatest things about being teen are freedom, friends, being young, and having fun," one 15-year-old girl told us.

"You're only young once, so you have to have as much fun now (without adult responsibilities) while you still can," said a 17-year-old boy.

Just under half of teens consider themselves innovative. The same proportion believe others see them as "cool." Those who agree with these statements are boldly confident in their peers' judgment of them.

The oldest teens are most comfortable with who they are. They are no longer trying to prove how "cool" or trendsetting they are. More of the younger teens (aged 12 to 17) have a "play now, pay later" attitude. Nearly half of those under age 18 say

# Teens Search for Identity

*Just under half of teens consider themselves innovative.*
*The same proportion believe others see them as "cool."*

**(percent of teens agreeing strongly/somewhat**
**with each statement, by age and gender, 1994)**

|  | total | aged 12-15 | | aged 16-17 | | aged 18-19 | |
|---|---|---|---|---|---|---|---|
|  |  | boys | girls | boys | girls | boys | girls |
| I always try to have as much fun as I possibly can—I don't know what the future holds and I don't care what others think. | 69% | 68% | 75% | 69% | 74% | 62% | 62% |
| I'm often the first to try something new. | 46 | 45 | 50 | 49 | 48 | 42 | 42 |
| Most people who know me or just see me think I'm cool. | 46 | 49 | 49 | 49 | 47 | 39 | 36 |

Source: TRU *Teenage Marketing & Lifestyle Study*

they are often the first to try something new and are perceived by others as "cool." Girls under age 18 are more likely than boys that age to think of themselves as carefree seekers of fun at any cost.

Minority teens are more likely than white teens to say that others think they're "cool." Sixty-three percent of African-Americans, 54 percent of Hispanics, and 41 percent of whites say others think they're "cool." Minority teens' perception that others think they are cool is supported by the fact that many white teens emulate their behavior.

There has been a gradual increase over the past few years in the percentage of teens who say they want to have fun at any cost. Conversely, a shrinking share of teens characterize themselves as innovative.

A pack mentality is apparent in the above data. Fewer teens feel they are striking out on their own, while more subscribe to the idea expressed by the 16-year-old boy who said, "Being an adult might suck, so I'm going to have as much fun now as I possibly can."

For marketers, these data suggest that teens will identify most with a portrayal of people their age as fun loving and fun seeking rather than as serious or stereotypically teen.

## The Serious Side

As much as teens just want to have fun, there's also a serious side to them. Nearly two out of three say that "it is very important to get involved in things that help others and help to make the world better, even if it's not important to others" their age. This serious attitude, while in contrast to the carefree mindset described above, adds another dimension to today's teens.

Teens in the late 1960s and early 1970s were more consumed with the politics and issues of the times. Teens in the 1980s were

# Changes in Identity Values

*There has been a gradual increase over the past few years in the percentage of teens who say they want to have fun at any cost.*

**(percent of teens agreeing strongly/somewhat with each statement, 1989-1993)**

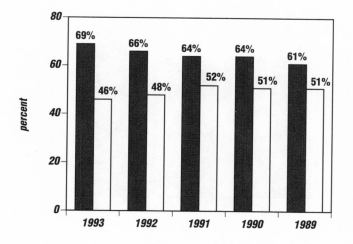

■ I always try to have as much fun as I possibly can—I don't know what the future holds and I don't care what others think.

☐ I'm often the first to try something new.

Source: TRU *Teenage Marketing & Lifestyle Study*

# Teens Get Serious

*Nearly two out of three teens want to make the world a better place, and half say religion is an important part of their lives.*

**(percent of teens agreeing strongly/somewhat with each statement, by gender, 1994)**

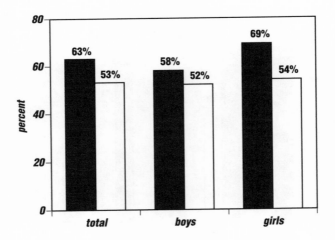

■ It's very important to me to get involved in things that help others and help to make the world better, even if it's not that important to others my age.

☐ My religion/faith is one of the most important parts of my life.

Source: TRU *Teenage Marketing & Lifestyle Study*

more driven by material concerns. Today's teens appear to be more balanced.

Most teens enjoy being with their families, for example. Their traditional values also include religion. More than half of teens say that "religion/faith is one of the most important parts" of their life.

African-American teens are more likely than either Hispanic or white teens to agree with the statements.

Although being religious and globally concerned continue to be important issues to most teens, agreement with both statements fell between 1992 and 1993. Among all teens, the proportion who think it is important to get involved fell from 69 to 63 percent. The proportion who agree that religion/faith is one of the most important parts of their life fell from 58 to 53 percent. As much as today's teens care about the world, what most excites them is fun. This shows why Pepsi's "have fun now" strategy was so timely and explains why it engaged so many teens.

## Great Expectations

Teens in the 1990s appear cautiously confident. Nearly seven out of ten say "things are really going well" for them and that they will always be successful. One in three hopes to live the same lifestyle that his or her parents live now.

The fact that only one-third of teens hope to live a similar lifestyle to that of their parents can be interpreted in a number of different ways. First, most teens want to live better (i.e., be more affluent) than their parents. Underscoring this interpretation is the fact that teens from lower-income homes are much less likely to say they hope to live a similar lifestyle as their parents. Second, some teens will not agree with this statement because of their own rebelliousness. As one commented, "When I'm my parents'

# Serious Values by Race and Ethnicity

*Religion is more important to African-American teens than it is to white or Hispanic teens.*

**(percent of teens agreeing strongly/somewhat with each statement, by race and ethnicity, 1994)**

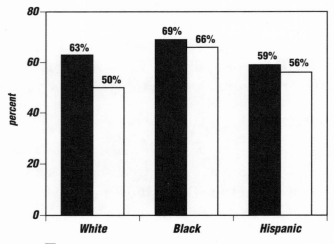

It's very important to me to get involved in things that help others and help to make the world better, even if it's not that important to others my age.

My religion/faith is one of the most important parts of my life.

Source: TRU *Teenage Marketing & Lifestyle Study*

174

age, I'm gonna make different choices. Even though you'll be an adult, you don't have to act like one." Significantly more boys (35 percent) than girls (31 percent) hope to live the same type of lifestyle as their parents.

Based on how teens see their current situation and their future, marketers who portray teen confidence and strength in advertising should find their message well received.

## Money Matters

Contrary to media reports that the American dream is dying, more than half of teens believe they will make more money in their lifetime than their parents will in theirs. At the same time, nearly one-third of teens say they personally have been affected by the recent recession. Many teens recognize the financial hardship their parents have been going through, and they think they can do better. Although economists predict that today's teens will be part of the first generation that will not exceed its parents in financial well-being, teens' own outlook is more optimistic. Some teens are aware of and accept such economic predictions, but most are confident that their own abilities, desire, and perseverance will help them beat the odds and exceed financially.

Teen boys are more likely to equate success with money than are teen girls, and older teens more so than younger teens. More African-Americans (45 percent) and Hispanic (46 percent) teens than white teens (32 percent) link success to making a lot of money.

Overall, teens of the 1990s are less materialistic than their predecessors in the 1980s. Sharply fewer equated success with money in 1993 than in 1987. But this anti-materialistic attitude peaked in 1991. Now the pendulum may be swinging back.

# Teens' Material Values

*More than half of teens believe they will make more money in their lifetime than their parents will in theirs.*

**(percent of teens agreeing strongly/somewhat with each statement, by gender and age, 1994)**

| | | gender | | age | | |
|---|---|---|---|---|---|---|
| | total | boys | girls | 12-15 | 16-17 | 18-19 |
| Earn more than parents | 56% | 62% | 49% | 54% | 61% | 55% |
| Success means money | 36 | 43 | 29 | 35 | 34 | 40 |
| Feel recession | 31 | 32 | 31 | 27 | 32 | 42 |

# Changes in Teens' Material Values

*Overall, teens of the 1990s are less materialistic than their predecessors in the 1980s.*

**(percent of teens agreeing strongly/somewhat that success means making a lot of money, 1987-1993)**

| | |
|---|---|
| 1993 | 36% |
| 1992 | 34 |
| 1991 | 32 |
| 1990 | 33 |
| 1989 | 38 |
| 1988 | 54 |

Source: TRU *Teenage Marketing & Lifestyle Study*

Even among teenagers, it's rare for attitudes to shift so much in just a few years. To understand this profound change, consider the events of the times. At the end of the 1980s, Communism fell in Eastern Europe. It was an event emphasized in school curricula and viewed as eye opening and relevant to American teens, many of whom had never before heard of the Berlin Wall or the Iron Curtain. "Channel One" was at the Wall interviewing German teenagers. The German teens' stories touched American teens in a relevant and heartfelt way. In our qualitative work during that time, teens continually brought up the subject, because it made them realize how important their freedom was to them. It was a concept, almost a revelation, that many teens had never before considered.

At about the same time, teens embraced the environmental movement, becoming more aware of this cause than they had been in the past. Finally, teens, like adults, rejected the excesses of the 1980s by turning away from materialism.

Regardless of the reasons for this shift, the message is clear. Although money is important to teens, it is less a priority than it once was. In marketing to teens, money and materialism are not the hot buttons they once were. Still, having enough money is one of teens' biggest everyday worries, making pricing and value-added strategies an important part of marketing to teens.

*Chapter Nine*

*The Essence of Being Teen*

**W**hat is it like being an American teenager in the 1990s? What are teens' hopes, worries, and motivations? What do they like and dislike about their current life stage? How old do teens really want to be? In what ways do they feel misunderstood? The answers to these questions reveal attitudes that are uniquely teen. Understanding teens' unique attitudes can spell the difference between developing products and marketing strategies that teens respect or alienating an entire cohort of consumers.

## The Meaning of "Cool"

As much as teens at times discount the importance of being cool, it remains the most deeply entrenched teen motivation. The teen need for belonging and acceptance are the psychological underpinnings for wanting to be cool. Since being cool is rooted in these psychological needs, it can be teens' overriding motivation, driving many of their behaviors—from socializing to purchasing.

The way teens determine who or what is cool reveals their innermost motivations, insecurities, and peer values. By knowing how teens define cool and recognizing the importance of cool as a working concept, you can choose talent and portray teens and young adults in advertising more effectively. By showing cool teens using your brand, you can benefit from a halo effect.

Several years ago, we undertook the process of defining cool from a teenage perspective. We started qualitatively, talking to teens one-on-one and in focus groups. We found that cool means different things to different teens, but it was universally regarded as being incredibly important. From our qualitative research, we compiled a list of attributes that some teens equate with cool. Then we asked respondents in our quantitative study:

# What Makes a Person Cool?

*An attractive physical appearance is the one attribute teens are most likely to associate with being cool.*

**(percent of teens associating attribute with being cool, 1993)**

|  | *percent* |
|---|---|
| Good looking | 52% |
| Has lots of friends | 40 |
| Popular with opposite sex | 36 |
| Outgoing personality | 34 |
| Funny | 34 |
| Good athlete | 28 |
| How he/she dresses | 26 |
| Smart | 19 |
| Big partyer | 15 |
| Independent | 13 |
| Owns cool stuff | 10 |
| Rebellious | 9 |

Source: TRU *Teenage Marketing & Lifestyle Study*

# Teen Boys and Girls Differ on What Makes a Person Cool

*Girls are more likely than boys to cite "good looking,"*
*"outgoing personality," and "how he/she dresses."*
*Boys place more weight on being "funny"*
*and a "good athlete."*

**(percent of teens who associate attribute with being cool, by gender, 1993)**

|                      | *boys* | *girls* |
|----------------------|--------|---------|
| Good looking         | 46%    | 58%     |
| Outgoing personality | 27     | 42      |
| Funny                | 36     | 32      |
| Good athlete         | 37     | 19      |
| How he/she dresses   | 22     | 30      |

Source: TRU *Teenage Marketing & Lifestyle Study*

"Think about somebody your age who's considered very cool. What makes that person so cool?"

If you think back to your own teenage years, then you probably know the answer to this question. Although teen preferences and lifestyles change over time, the number-one criterion of being cool has not changed: good looks. An attractive physical appearance is the one attribute teens are most likely to associate with cool. This finding is good news for the marketers of health and beauty aids. The motivation to look good is as strong as ever, central to the way teens feel about themselves and a key component in driving teen consumer behavior.

When you're in high school, then, you can get by almost on looks alone, according to these data. I've talked to many adults who reminisce about the best-looking girl or boy in their high school (also usually the most popular) who hasn't achieved much since then (typically to their delight!).

But, as teens age, their definition of cool matures. Among 18- and 19-year-olds, as many say an outgoing personality is cool as say "good looks" are cool.

"The coolest kids at school are those who are the most fun to be around," said a 19-year-old boy in one of our focus groups.

"There are a lot of cool people at college, and it seems like they are the ones who have the most friends," commented an 18-year-old girl.

The second and third most frequently cited attributes associated with cool are popularity measures: having lots of friends and being popular with the opposite sex. Fourth is having an outgoing personality, while fifth is being funny. These top-five descriptors of cool are interdependent. If someone is good-looking, he or she is more likely to be popular with the opposite sex, and this increases his or her popularity among same-gender friends.

Good looks has always been one of the most important attributes associated with cool. But other attributes have waxed and waned over the years. Being independent, a partyer, and rebellious probably would have ranked much higher 20 years ago. Today, being rebellious is cited as an attribute of cool by only 9 percent of teens, probably because there is less for teens to rebel against these days. Today's teens feel less of a generation gap with their parents than previous teen cohorts, nor do they feel alienated from society. In fact, "system" and "society" are two words we seldom hear teens use these days. Finally, it's simply more challenging to be rebellious in these days of almost-anything goes.

In contrast, the attribute of "being a good dresser" probably would have been considered superficial by teens 20 years ago. It certainly would have ranked below being independent or rebellious.

Boys and girls place different priorities on some cool attributes. Girls are more likely than boys to cite "good looking," "outgoing personality," and "how he/she dresses." Boys place more weight on being "funny" and a "good athlete." There were no significant differences in the responses of boys and girls to "big partyer," "independent," "rebellious," "has lots of friends," or "popular with opposite sex."

## Teens and Age Aspiration

A few years ago I attended a youth-marketing conference in which a speaker discussed the critical issue of taking into account age aspiration: communicating and appealing to teens based on the age they aspire to rather than their current age.

# How Old Teens Want to Be

*On average, 12-year-olds want to be 17, literally skipping over most of their teen years.*

**(teens' actual age and the age they aspire to, in years, 1992)**

| actual age | aspired age | gap in years |
|---|---|---|
| 12 | 17 | 5 |
| 13 | 18 | 5 |
| 14 | 18 | 4 |
| 15 | 18 | 3 |
| 16 | 19 | 3 |
| 17 | 20 | 3 |
| 18 | 20 | 2 |
| 19 | 20 | 1 |

Source: TRU *Teenage Marketing & Lifestyle Study*

She explained that young teens want to be 16, while 16-year-olds want to be 18, and 18-year-olds want to be 21. After her presentation, I asked her where she got her data, since it seemed about right and it was an issue we were also exploring at TRU. Her findings, she said, were based on her observations and on talking informally with kids, the same sources we had been relying on to arrive at a similar hypothesis.

By happenstance, we were going to send the questionnaire for our twice-a-year syndicated survey to the printer the next day. But we were able to squeeze in one final question: "If you could be any age right now, what age would you be?"

The results show that the question was well worth asking. On average, 12-year-olds want to be 17, literally skipping over most of their teen years! Although perhaps startling, this finding makes sense. These youngest teens watch their older brothers and sisters, the upper classmen in their schools, the older kids in the neighborhood, and older teens (typically portrayed by twentysomethings!) in TV and movies. As they watch, they think, "Wow, they're having more fun than me. They're driving, dating, even their faces are clearing up!"

By the time teens reach age 18 or 19, they're thinking, "Hey, I have it pretty good right now. Not a lot of responsibility, but a lot of independence. I think I'd like to be just a year or two older." Older teens are in no particular hurry to enter the adult world of serious responsibilities. They're pleased with the balance they have achieved between adult freedoms and teen fun.

The gap in teens' actual age and the age they aspire to be shrinks as they get older. The youngest teens (12- to 15-year-olds) aspire to be three to five years older than they are. They are less content with their current life stage and love to imagine themselves older, actually longing to see the aging process accelerated. Younger teens look forward to the independence and greater variety of activities that come with maturity, such as driving, dating, working, going to college, and moving out. Older teens are more content with their current age, enjoying all the things younger teens yearn to do.

The message to marketers is one of strategic convenience. In positioning a product or brand, aim high in the tone of your message and any talent you choose to portray it. Talk to older teens, since younger ones aspire to their level. This is good news, since few brands have marketing budgets that allow for segmenting the teen market by age.

These findings can also help guide you in deciding upon the age of the actors to use in teen-directed advertising. If your target is 12-to-15-year-olds, consider using 17-year-old actors. You'll grab the youngest teens because they aspire to be like the actor. At the same time, the ads will still appeal to 16- and 17-year-olds because they will identify with people their own age, allowing you to appeal to a broader age target.

## What Teens Like About Being Teen

TRU's studies show that despite the pressures and obstacles teens face, most enjoy this life stage. We recently asked our teen sample this question: "Do you like being a teenager?" Nearly 90 percent said yes.

This does not mean that teens are trouble-free. Still, the data clearly show that teens rate their current life stage as more enjoyable than not. Not surprisingly, however, the oldest teens are somewhat less satisfied with being a teenager than are their younger counterparts. Older teens are troubled with adult stereotyping of their age group. They have been teen long enough. So they are tiring of this life stage and await the greater independence they associate with being an adult.

# What Teens Like Most About Being Teen

*Teens cite close friends and having a boyfriend/girlfriend as what they most like about being teen.*

**(percent of teens citing factor as what they like about being teen, 1993)**

|  | *percent* |
|---|---|
| Close friends | 32% |
| Boyfriend/girlfriend | 25 |
| Freedom | 24 |
| Partying | 24 |
| Not getting caught | 19 |
| Able to drive | 17 |
| No adult responsibility | 14 |
| Dating | 14 |
| School events | 13 |
| Going to school | 9 |
| Few worries | 8 |
| Few expectations | 6 |

Source: TRU *Teenage Marketing & Lifestyle Study*

We also asked respondents what they like about being teen. Reflecting the importance of social relationships in their lives, teens cite close friends and having a boyfriend/girlfriend as what they most like about being teen. Other findings from TRU research confirm the paramount importance of friends to teens. For example, teens say they would rather have a guaranteed great time with their friends than with their family. Teens turn most often to their friends for advice. They depend on their friends to cue them in on the latest trends, and they place tremendous importance on having a couple of close friends.

"Friends are the best part [about being teen]. We always have a great time together and they're there when you can't talk to your parents," said one 14-year-old girl.

"Freedom" and "partying" rank second and third among the best things about being a teen. Both involve social interaction: teens enjoy the freedom to be with friends and away from their family, and they especially like to "party" with friends. (Of course, "partying" means different things to different teens.)

"The greatest thing is that we're old enough to do a lot of things while not having adult responsibilities to worry about," said a 16-year-old boy.

"Being able to do what you want is great; adults can't act stupid like teens can," commented a 15-year-old girl.

"Being a teen is great because you're able to have fun, be with friends, party without having to worry about much," said a 16-year-old girl.

Nearly 20 percent of teens say their favorite part of being teen is "doing things you're not supposed to and not getting caught." Younger teens are slightly more rebellious in this way than their older counterparts: 22 percent of 12-to-15-year-olds

# What Boys and Girls Like Most About Being Teen

*Girls are more likely than boys to cite "close friends" and "not getting caught" as the best things about being teen. Boys are more likely to cite "being able to drive."*

**(top five factors teens like about being teen, percent citing by gender, 1993)**

|  | *percent* |
|---|---|
| **Boys** | |
| Close friends | 28% |
| Freedom | 26 |
| Partying | 25 |
| Having a girlfriend | 22 |
| Able to drive | 19 |
| **Girls** | |
| Close friends | 36 |
| Having a boyfriend | 29 |
| Partying | 23 |
| Freedom | 22 |
| Not getting caught | 21 |

Source: TRU *Teenage Marketing & Lifestyle Study*

said this versus 18 percent of 16-to-19-year-olds. Perhaps older teens have been getting away with deviant behavior for a few years, so it is no longer as exciting as it once was. Younger teens, on the other hand, are still in the early stages of experimenting with pushing the limits of independence.

To some teens, "partying" overlaps with "doing things you're not supposed to." Thirty-seven percent of teens cite one of these responses, revealing how appealing it is to teens to do things their parents may frown upon.

"Being a teen is great because you can do whatever you want and not get caught," said a 15-year-old boy.

"I like being able to fool around, being lazy and free, and doing things behind my parents' backs and not getting caught," said a 16-year-old girl. There are significant gender differences on this measure. Girls are more likely than boys to cite "close friends" and "not getting caught" as the best things about being teen. Boys are more likely to cite "being able to drive."

These likes also vary by age. More younger (12 to 15) than older (16 to 19) teens cite "dating" and "not getting caught." Teens aged 16 and 17 are most likely to name "driving" or "not having adult responsibilities." These teens have just gotten their driver's license and are enjoying greater freedom and independence because of it. They're also beginning to recognize the responsibilities that come with adulthood and have a greater appreciation for their relatively carefree lifestyle. Significantly more 18- and 19-year-olds than 12-to-17-year-olds mention "freedom" as what they most like about being teen. Many of these young adults are on their own for the first time, either at college or in the work force.

## What Teens Dislike About Being Teen

TRU also asked respondents what they dislike about being teen. By understanding what teens (and teen segments) dislike most about their current life stage, marketers can offer solutions and empathy for the problems teens face.

When asked, "What do you most dislike about being a teenager?" more teens name "peer pressure" than anything else.

"Peer pressure ... because you don't act yourself. You try to be someone you're not just to try to please someone else," said a 17-year-old girl in a focus group.

"Peer pressure. Almost every teenager is pressured into alcohol, drugs, sex, etcetera. Many people want to try to fit in, and they will ruin their life to fit in," said a 14-year-old girl.

"Trying to resist peer pressure. If there wasn't so much pressure, many teens would make it through life a lot easier," commented an 18-year-old girl.

"Peer pressure makes you go against your beliefs sometimes. It's really hard to say 'no' when you want to 'fit in' so bad," said a 15-year-old boy.

"There's a lot of peer pressure; there are always people trying to change you and make you fit in with them, especially about joining a gang," said a 16-year-old boy.

"It's really hard sometimes being a teen because you're constantly being judged by what you do, wear, or what type of music you listen to," complained a 14-year-old girl.

Peer pressure is omnipresent, motivating, and punishing. It affects teen decisions far beyond what brand of jeans they wear or what soda they drink. Today, it influences teen involvement in sex, drinking, drugs, and gangs. Younger teens are most affected

# What Teens Dislike Most About Being Teen

*More teens name "peer pressure" than anything else.*

**(percent of teens citing factor as what they dislike about being teen, 1993)**

|  | *percent* |
|---|---|
| Peer pressure | 33% |
| Not taken seriously | 23 |
| Not enough money | 21 |
| Age restrictions | 19 |
| Parent pressures | 19 |
| Lack of respect | 17 |
| Grades | 15 |
| Curfew | 14 |
| Going to school | 13 |
| Parent hassles | 12 |
| Physical changes | 11 |
| Worrying about fitting in | 11 |
| Standardized tests | 9 |
| Too much responsibility | 7 |
| Trends change fast | 6 |
| Treated badly at stores | 5 |

Source: TRU *Teenage Marketing & Lifestyle Study*

by peer pressure. Older teens, who have more experience with peer pressure, cope with it more easily.

The second biggest complaint about being teen is not being taken seriously. Significantly more older teens (18 and 19) cite this than do younger teens. Twenty-nine percent of 18- and 19-year-olds complain that they are not taken seriously, versus 26 percent of 16- and 17-year-olds and 19 percent of 12-to-15-year-olds. Twenty-seven percent of 18- and 19-year-olds say the worst part of being teen is age restrictions. Our qualitative research has found that older teens often feel frustrated with their "in between" status. They believe themselves to be mature and responsible—sometimes more mature than the adults around them.

"I can tell you when I drink with my friends, I'm a lot more responsible than some of my parents' friends," said an 18-year-old boy.

"The worst part about being teen is not being old enough to do some things, but being old enough to do others. It's difficult to figure out what we can and can't do," said a 15-year-old boy.

"It's tough dealing with the transition from child to adult. You're not really accepted by the adult community because you're not old enough, but you're too old to act like a child. Sometimes it's really frustrating," complained a 15-year-old girl.

The third-ranking teen dislike is a universal problem: not having enough money. Many teens, especially younger ones, rely almost exclusively on an allowance and parental handouts for spending money. Although most of teens' income is discretionary, many feel pressure to keep up with the latest fashion and entertainment trends, which can be expensive. Money is an important part of teens' social lives. As teens have told us, "not having the funds" can seriously hamper their romantic aspirations.

Teens feel pressure not only from peers but also from parents. Nineteen percent name "pressure from parents" as one of the things they most dislike about being a teenager.

"Having your parents always telling you what to do" is how one 13-year-old boy put it.

A 19-year-old girl explained that she disliked "the pressure from parents to act older and mature. But at the same time, they treat you like a little kid."

"Parents are always trying to get you to be what they want you to be rather than what you want to be," said a 17-year-old boy.

Separately, another 12 percent complain about "parent hassles." Overall, 26 percent of teens name either parent pressure or parent hassles. Although there is less of a generation gap today than a generation ago, teens and parents still struggle to get along.

"Parents expect you to read their minds! They want you to do something, but they don't tell you to do it. Then, they yell at you for not doing it!" said a 15-year-old girl.

"Parents are a hassle. They're too pushy, overprotective, bossy, nosy, and they don't let you do anything," said a 16-year-old girl.

"It's really hard trying to get parents to understand why you do things. They always say, 'We never did that when we were your age.' It's like, who cares?" said a 13-year-old girl.

"Parents—you can't live with them, you can't live without them!" exclaimed a 15-year-old boy.

Significantly more girls than boys name "peer pressure" (28 percent vs. 24 percent) and "physical changes" (15 percent vs. 8

percent) as dislikes, while significantly more boys name "going to school" (16 percent vs. 10 percent).

"The toughest thing about being teen is what you look like because no guy wants to go out with an ugly girl and no girl wants to be around an unpopular girl," said a 12-year-old girl.

"It's hard going through all of these physical changes, like acne and reaching 'maturity,'" complained another 12-year-old girl.

"School is tough. There's so much to worry about, like grades, homework, and tests. And, you have to get past [school] in order to do anything else," said a 14-year-old boy.

## Teen Expectations and Hopes

TRU regularly asks teens about their hopes and expectations. By understanding teen hopes and expectations, you gain insight into what teens feel about the future. This gives you the opportunity to talk to teens about their dreams, communicating with them in a relevant and compelling way. Our studies show that teens expect to have a traditional adult life (own a home, marry, have a successful career, have children). But they hope for a more glamorous lifestyle, marked by wealth, travel, and fame.

What teens are most likely to expect in their adult lives they least hope for, and what they most hope for is what they least expect. Teens envision leading the same adult lifestyle as their parents. They expect to marry, have children, and buy a home. In fact, more than eight out of ten expect to own a home. Not only do teens think owning a home is the norm (without fully understanding what buying a home entails), they're also optimistic (perhaps, naively so) about their financial ability to buy a home in the future.

# Teen Expectations and Hopes

*Teens expect to have a traditional adult life, but they hope for a more glamorous lifestyle, marked by wealth, travel, and fame.*

**(percent of teens citing what they expect in their adult life and percent citing what they hope for in their adult life, 1992)**

|  | *expect* | *hope* |
|---|---|---|
| Own home | 84% | 48% |
| Marry | 73 | 50 |
| Successful career | 70 | 61 |
| Children | 68 | 49 |
| A lot of money | 48 | 71 |
| World travel | 23 | 64 |
| Fame | 15 | 58 |

Source: TRU *Teenage Marketing & Lifestyle Study*

A majority of teens to marry and have children, but few *hope* to marry and have children. At this stage in their lives, when they're struggling with their parents, they can't relate to the idea of having their own family someday. Yet, they expect to follow society's norm of marrying and having children.

Because teens find realistic advertising most appealing, you should incorporate teens' real expectations and hopes into your marketing. Teens will respond favorably to advertising that offers them the opportunity to realize their hopes, rather than simply meet their expectations.

It's critically important to avoid portraying the future as offering no more than marriage and children. Marriage, parenthood, and home ownership are too mundane and too distant to appeal to teens contemplating their futures and dreaming of excitement and glamour.

I recently conducted some one-on-one interviews with male high-school athletes to check the effectiveness of the communication in a new advertising campaign for one of the major athletic footwear companies. Not only did two of the boys tell me that someday they would appear in these commercials, they genuinely believed it! You would think these guys would recognize that the odds against their achieving sports celebrity were astronomical. But they wanted to believe in it. Creating advertising that balances what teens long for with what they find believable is a real challenge in marketing to teens.

## What Teens Look Forward To

While it is important to understand what teens think about their future as adults, it's also important to know what they look forward to doing in the near future.

# What Teens Most Look Forward To

*Graduation is the most frequently cited event, followed by summer, getting a driver's license, going to college, and getting a job.*

**(percent of teens citing event as something they look forward to, 1993)**

| | *percent* |
|---|---|
| Graduating | 29% |
| Summer | 24 |
| Driver's license | 23 |
| College | 21 |
| Job | 18 |
| College acceptance | 16 |
| Vacation/travel | 16 |
| Starting career | 15 |
| More freedom | 14 |
| Moving out | 13 |
| Prom | 9 |
| Athletic event | 8 |
| Weekends | 8 |
| Adult responsibility | 6 |
| Fraternity/sorority | 2 |

Source: TRU *Teenage Marketing & Lifestyle Study*

# What Teens Look Forward to Differs by Age

*The closer in age a teenager is to a specific event or milestone, the more eagerly he or she awaits the event.*

**(percent of teens citing event as something they look forward to, by age, 1993)**

|  | *12-15* | *16-17* | *18-19* |
|---|---|---|---|
| Graduating | 30% | 40% | 17% |
| Summer | 27 | 25 | 18 |
| Getting driver's license | 35 | 16 | 3 |
| Going to college | 16 | 25 | 26 |
| Getting a job | 20 | 17 | 16 |
| College acceptance | 19 | 21 | 4 |
| Vacation/travel | 18 | 11 | 16 |
| Starting career | 11 | 11 | 27 |
| Having more freedom | 16 | 15 | 9 |
| Moving out | 9 | 12 | 20 |

Source: TRU *Teenage Marketing & Lifestyle Study*

In focus groups, we asked teens to list events, occasions, or situations that they were looking forward to doing. We then asked our national sample of teenagers to select the one or two things from this list of 15 that they most eagerly anticipate doing.

Graduation is the most frequently cited event, followed by summer, getting a driver's license, going to college, and getting a job. Teens are most excited about quickly approaching milestones because it's easier for them to visualize an event close to them than one that is more distant. Because of this, it is essential to view these data by age group. Fourteen-year-olds look forward to very different events than 19-year-olds.

Unlike the age-aspiration measure, which varies little by age, the results of this measure are not as convenient for marketing applications. Clearly, teens are short-term thinkers! The closer in age a teenager is to a specific event or milestone, the more eagerly he or she awaits the event. The results of this measure point out relevant events and life stage experiences that can be incorporated into advertising or promotions to appeal to each teenage segment. The event that is most imminent in the target segment's life is likely to prove the most motivating.

## Adults' Biggest Misconceptions About Teens

Teens commonly complain that their parents "just don't understand us." Teens feel that adults think they are all alike, relying on stereotypes to describe them. Although parents can survive a guilty verdict on this measure, advertisers cannot.

Through a series of focus groups, we crafted a list of 14 adult misconceptions about teens, according to teens. Then we quantified the list in our large national study.

According to teens, the biggest misconception adults have about people their age is that they are not mature enough to

# Biggest Adult Misconceptions About Teens

*According to teens, the biggest misconception adults have about people their age is that they are not mature enough to handle responsibility.*

**(percent of teens citing factor as a big adult misconception about teens, 1994)**

|  | *percent* |
|---|---|
| Not mature enough | 52% |
| Cause trouble | 47 |
| Lazy | 35 |
| No problems/worries | 29 |
| Take drugs | 25 |
| Not intelligent | 24 |
| Lack commitment | 23 |
| Watch too much TV | 22 |
| Don't strive | 22 |
| Sexually active | 21 |
| Bad drivers | 21 |
| Unconcerned about world | 20 |
| In gangs | 19 |
| Drink alcohol | 16 |

Source: TRU *Teenage Marketing & Lifestyle Study*

# Teen Boys and Girls Agree on Adult Misconceptions About Teens

*More boys than girls think adults assume teens take drugs, while more girls than boys believe adults assume teens are sexually active.*

**(percent of teens citing factor as a big adult misconception about teens, by gender, 1994)**

| | *percent* |
|---|---|
| **Boys** | |
| Cause trouble | 52% |
| Not mature enough to handle responsibility | 49 |
| Lazy | 37 |
| Take drugs | 28 |
| No problems, worries | 27 |
| **Girls** | |
| Not mature enough to handle responsibility | 56 |
| Cause trouble | 43 |
| Lazy | 34 |
| No problems, worries | 32 |
| Sexually active | 24 |

Source: TRU *Teenage Marketing & Lifestyle Study*

handle responsibility. Interestingly, 19-year-olds are just as likely as 12-year-olds to feel this way. This finding underscores how important it is for teens to believe advertisers respect their intelligence, or, to put it in teen vernacular, that companies do not "diss" them.

"One of the worst parts about being teen is having people think you're not mature or responsible enough to do things when you know you can," said a 14-year-old girl.

Many teens resent the fact that adults view teens as trouble-makers. In focus groups, teens complain about the small but vocal minority of people their age who cause adults to write off the entire age group.

"There's a few troublemakers in school who give all of us a bad name," said a 15-year-old girl.

"You are always getting compared to the negative statistics of teens, and it puts a limit on your privileges," commented a 14-year-old girl.

"The toughest thing about being teen is making adults understand that all teens are not alike. We're not all under a bad influence," said a 19-year-old girl.

"Since most adults think all teens are on drugs and in gangs, they don't give credit to those teens who are doing their best to stay away from that stuff," said a 17-year-old boy.

Being immature and causing trouble are not the only stereo-types that teens find troubling. Teens rank being lazy as the third-biggest misconception, followed by not having problems or worries. None of the top-four misconceptions focus on a specific behavior (such as taking drugs or drinking alcohol). Perhaps these general attitudes are most bothersome to teens because they're the hardest to disprove. Either someone does or does not do drugs. It's much more difficult to combat the image of immaturity, irresponsibility, or laziness.

"I hate it when adults stereotype all teens as being lazy and trouble makers," complained a 16-year-old girl.

"Adults think teens don't have problems and worries but we do. There's a lot of pressure to 'fit in' and we worry about getting into a good school and our futures," said a 17-year-old boy.

Not surprisingly, there are some gender differences worth noting on the misconception measure. Four of the top five misconceptions are cited by both boys and girls. But more boys than girls think adults assume teens take drugs, while more girls than boys believe adults assume teens are sexually active. Significantly more younger than older teens feel that adults assume teens cause trouble, are lazy, and watch too much TV. Conversely, more older teens say adults assume teens don't have problems and that they lack commitment.

Significantly more minority teens than white teens say taking drugs, causing trouble, and being in gangs are adult misconceptions. Significantly more white teens, on the other hand, say adults believe teens watch too much TV and are not mature enough to handle responsibility.

## Biggest Everyday Worries

One of the biggest misconceptions teens say adults have about them is that they don't have problems or worries. But, teens worry a lot. They worry about everything from grades and planning their future to performing well in sports and wearing the right clothes. These worries can be leveraged in advertising to teens. Though teens will tell you that they care about issues like AIDS or saving the earth, they are motivated more by how they

# Biggest Everyday Worries of Teens

*Although teens will tell you that they care about issues like AIDS or saving the earth, they are motivated more by how they look and whether they have cash in their pocket.*

**(percent of teens citing factor as a big worry, 1993)**

|  | *percent* |
|---|---|
| Grades | 52% |
| Having enough money | 48 |
| How you look | 47 |
| Planning your future | 38 |
| Getting along with parents | 30 |
| Being talked about behind your back | 27 |
| Having a boyfriend/girlfriend | 25 |
| Getting into college | 25 |
| Doing well at sports | 22 |
| Wearing the right clothes | 14 |
| Having a couple of really close friends | 13 |
| Having lots of friends | 12 |
| Being sexually active | 11 |
| Unplanned pregnancy | 10 |
| Being able to drive | 10 |
| Getting a date | 10 |
| Gangs | 9 |
| Being considered cool | 9 |
| Getting into trouble with authorities | 8 |

Source: TRU *Teenage Marketing & Lifestyle Study*

look and whether they have cash in their pocket. When we quantified teens' everyday worries, here's what we found.

Girls are bigger worriers than boys—they are more concerned about five of the top-six worries than are boys. While girls worry about everything from how they look to what people think about them, boys worry more than girls only about having enough money.

There are significant differences in everyday worries by age. Eighteen- and 19-year-olds are primarily concerned with "having enough money" and "planning your future." All other worries seem relatively unimportant to the oldest teens. "Grades" is the number-one concern among younger teens, especially 12- to-17-year-olds (18- and 19-year-olds are less concerned with grades because 20 percent of them are not in school), a finding consistent with the fact that 55 percent of teens say that studying is "in."

"If you don't get good grades now, it will affect the rest of your life," explained a 17-year-old boy.

Don't be misled by this finding. Just because grades are the biggest teen worry doesn't mean that most teens strive for academic excellence. There are other reasons grades are such a big concern, from being grounded by parents because of low grades to being ruled ineligible to play on sports teams. So, not making good grades can really cramp a teen's style.

Grades are also key because they are the single quantification of a student's progress—a measure with emotional, social, intellectual, and achievement ramifications. If you've ever awakened in the middle of the night in a cold sweat over a nightmare in which you failed to study for your high school history final, it shouldn't be difficult to understand the pressure on teens. It can consume them.

# Teen Boys and Girls Have Similar Worries

*While girls worry about everything from how they look to what people think about them, boys worry more than girls only about having enough money.*

**(percent of teens citing factor as a big worry, by gender, 1993)**

|  | *boys* | *girls* |
|---|---|---|
| Grades | 50% | 54% |
| Having enough money | 50 | 45 |
| How you look | 37 | 58 |
| Planning your future | 36 | 40 |
| Parents | 25 | 36 |
| Being talked about | 24 | 30 |

Source: TRU *Teenage Marketing & Lifestyle Study*

"Man, if it weren't for grades, I'd like to stay a student forever," said a 15-year-old boy.

"Grades are like a constant gun pointed at your head," said a 14-year-old girl.

After grades, the youngest teens are most concerned with how they look (53 percent), particularly 12-to-15-year-old girls (63 percent). Girls in this age group are 17 percentage points more likely than 16-to-17-year-old girls and 26 percentage points more likely than 18-to-19-year-old girls to say "how you look" is one of their biggest everyday worries. This finding is consistent with our Teen Value Monitor measure showing that girls aged 12 to 15 are the most insecure about how others perceive them.

Another big worry for the youngest teens is "people talking about you behind your back." In fact, this is the third-biggest worry for 12-to-15-year-old girls, and it's anything but new to teens. Generations of teenagers have shared the same concern, and it's connected to the stage of maturation. Teens who are going through puberty, or who recently went though puberty, are most concerned about being talked about.

This concern offers some potent leverage for advertisers, particularly those with products that can aid teens during this physiological transition. Teens buy acne treatments that they think will most effectively prevent or eliminate acne. They buy brands of clothing that are most accepted by their peer group. Once teens find products they trust, they are hesitant to abandon them for others. Since teens are consumed with concern about their physical appearance, if you can offer teens improved or "no-risk" looks you're sure to strike a responsive chord.

"One big worry for teens is what other people think of you. If someone who is popular says something bad about you, everyone starts talking about you," said a 12-year-old girl.

# Teen Worries
# Differ by Age

*Grades is the number-one concern among younger teens, especially 12-to-17-year-olds.*

**(percent of teens citing factor as a big worry, by age, 1993)**

|  | *percent* |
|---|---|
| **Aged 12-15** | |
| Grades | 57% |
| Looks | 53 |
| Money | 39 |
| Talk behind back | 34 |
| Getting along with parents | 32 |
| **Aged 16-17** | |
| Grades | 55 |
| Money | 48 |
| Future | 47 |
| Looks | 43 |
| Getting into college | 39 |
| **Aged 18-19** | |
| Money | 66 |
| Future | 63 |
| Looks | 39 |
| Grades | 37 |
| Getting along with parents | 26 |

Source: TRU *Teenage Marketing & Lifestyle Study*

"There's a lot of pressure about who your friends are because if they're not really your friends, they'll talk about you behind your back," said a 15-year-old boy.

Clearasil had been running a highly successful campaign, leveraging these teen fears of being talked about behind their backs combined with the even bigger worry of "how you look." One TV spot showed a girl holding up a red polka-dotted white sheet, asking her friends the question, "Whose face does this remind you of?" She and her friends reply in unison by yelling out the unfortunate boy's name. Naturally, in the course of 30 seconds the boy's face clears up and he gets the girl! When we ask teens about this spot, many say it's mean. In the same breath, however, they say it's "real." The campaign evolved with less harsh executions, which kept the advertising fresh and effective.

## Whom Do Teens Most Admire?

The question of how to motivate teens is crucial not only for marketers, but also for teachers, counselors, and social-service agencies and other organizations that support young people. Knowing who teens look up to can be a starting point in motivating teens. By portraying in advertising the type of people teens (or a teen segment) admire, you can make your advertising message more compelling.

To determine whom teens admire, we asked in our syndicated study: "Thinking about somebody whom you really admire—or who even may be a hero to you—which of the following best identifies that person?" Then we presented them with a list of 20 choices, from "mother" to "historical figure" to "social leader." Separately, we asked them to identify the specific individual they most admire and explain why.

The results reveal teens' strong admiration and affection for their families. The top two answers are mother and father, respectively.

"My mother. She works full-time and raises a family of four and loves us all and is sweet and understanding," said a 16-year-old girl.

"My dad. He is my best friend," said a 13-year-old boy.

We asked teens this question in our very first syndicated study in 1983. Then, too, teens most admired their parents. The implications of this finding are challenging to advertisers. As much as teens want separation from their parents, they may reject advertising that is overly insulting to parents. Humor can be an effective way to straddle this contradiction.

Advertising that shows the importance of parents as role models can be motivating to teens. Teens found one execution of Levi's 501 brand's "Got to Be Real" campaign, focusing on a Native American boy, to be especially moving. The young teen says, "I don't know of any friends who have fathers like mine. He's just one of the greatest guys you can know." His father is shown sitting in the background, smiling subtly but proudly in response to hearing his son's thoughts.

Although parents are viewed as admirably today as they were more than a decade ago, teachers are not. In 1983, teachers were right behind mom and dad as the people teens most admired. The new data show that teachers have fallen off the charts. This same finding emerges when we ask teens whom they would turn to first if they needed personal advice. Again, teachers rank low on this measure, indicating that today's education system (as represented by teachers) has fallen sharply in teens' estimation over the past ten years.

Celebrities have replaced teachers as the people teens most admire after mom and dad. Third is "sports stars," fourth is "musical performers, and fifth is teens themselves. The fact that "yourself" scored as high as it did reflects the confidence that a minority of teens have in themselves.

"Myself. I don't try to be someone else. I do what I want to do, not what someone else wants me to do," said a 16-year-old girl.

"Magic Johnson. Even though he has AIDS, he had the guts to tell us, and now he can teach others about AIDS. He isn't a big shot; he cares and doesn't want others to do what he did," said a 12-year-old boy.

"My parents. They trust people until those people give them a reason not to," said a 17-year-old girl.

Just as revealing as the top choices are the bottom three: current political figure, boss, and scientist. Clearly, these figures should be used only humorously in advertising to teens.

Responses to this question vary by gender, but not significantly by age. Teens are most likely to admire people of the same gender. Girls are much more likely than boys to admire mom (28 vs. 13 percent) or a sister. Boys are more likely than girls to admire dad (20 vs. 10 percent) or a sports star (23 vs. 4 percent). In fact, boys are more likely to admire a sports star than dad. Said one 17-year-old boy: "Michael Jordan. He is everything you would want to be: rich, popular, good looking, and in control."

"My mother. She is hard working, and she is always teaching me things that I need to survive in the future. She is always there when I need her. She is like a sister and a best friend to me. She teaches me to be independent," said an 18-year-old girl.

"Madonna. Because even after all is said and done, she gets back on her feet and fights. She takes steps that others wouldn't take to make herself happy," said a 17-year-old girl.

"Martin Luther King Jr. and Malcolm X. They stood up against adversity and made life for blacks a little easier," said a 14-year-old boy.

"Angel Martino. She's a great swimmer who overcame attacks by the press and suspension for steroids, which was never proven," said a 14-year-old girl.

## To Whom Do Teens Turn for Advice?

For some products, depicting an advice giver in advertising can be especially effective. This is particularly true for health and beauty aids. To help you decide whom you should picture in an advice-giver role, we ask teens: "Who is the first person you turn to when you need advice about a personal problem?"

By a significant margin, the number-one answer is a friend, mentioned by more than half of teens. Second is mother, followed by girlfriend or boyfriend, and father.

Of course, the nature of the problem will determine whom a teen turns to for advice. If the problem is, "I need help with algebra," a teen probably would turn to a parent. If the problem is, "I'm thinking about having sex with a particular person," teens are more likely to turn to their friends for advice. It's only the rare (and fortunate) parents whose teenaged children would come first to them if struggling with this issue.

Teens are more likely to turn to their friends for advice than anyone else for a variety of reasons. The problem they have may be too controversial or risky to broach with parents; a friend may have recently experienced a similar situation; and sometimes it's

# Where Teens Go for Advice

*The number-one answer is a friend, mentioned by more than half of teens. Second is mother, followed by girlfriend or boyfriend, and father.*

**(percent of teens saying they would turn for advice to the following persons/services, 1993)**

|  | *percent* |
|---|---|
| Friend | 55% |
| Mother | 44 |
| Boyfriend/girlfriend | 23 |
| Father | 20 |
| Sister | 10 |
| Other family member | 7 |
| Brother | 7 |
| Teacher | 4 |
| School counselor | 3 |
| Coach | 3 |
| Magazine/newspaper | 2 |
| Clergy | 2 |
| Psychologist/social worker | 1 |
| Medical doctor | 1 |
| Crisis hotline | 1 |

Source: TRU *Teenage Marketing & Lifestyle Study*

# Where Teen Boys and Girls Go for Advice

*Teenage boys are more likely than girls to go to their father or brother for advice, while girls are more likely to turn to friends, mom, girlfriends, or sisters.*

**(percent of teens citing selected persons as the one they would turn to for advice, by gender, 1993)**

|                     | *boys* | *girls* |
|---------------------|--------|---------|
| Friend              | 48%    | 63%     |
| Mother              | 41     | 48      |
| Boyfriend/girlfriend| 19     | 26      |
| Father              | 30     | 9       |
| Sister              | 8      | 12      |
| Brother             | 10     | 3       |

Source: TRU *Teenage Marketing & Lifestyle Study*

more comfortable talking with someone who is not an authority figure.

Teenage boys are more likely than girls to go to their father or brother for advice, while girls are more likely to turn to friends, mom, girlfriends, or sisters. Dad ranks relatively low on this measure, for several reasons. First, many teens today come from single-parent homes headed by their mother; they don't have a dad close by to turn to for advice. Second, even if teens live with both parents, dad is often less accessible than mom. Finally, in focus groups, teens tell us that they think their mother is more interested in their problems and more nurturing in her response than is their father.

Nearly 25 percent of teens say they turn to their boyfriend or girlfriend for advice. If the data were based only on respondents who have a boyfriend or girlfriend, the percentage would probably double. This shows just how important boyfriends and girlfriends are in sharing problems and giving advice.

Adult authority figures outside the family, such as teachers, coaches, counselors, or clergy, all rank low as advice givers. Teens also rank outside services, such as crisis lines, low. Of course, the only teens who would turn to crisis lines would be those with major problems.

## Friends or Family: A Hypothetical Question

Most teens say they enjoy being with their families. But the question is, compared to what? To find the answer, we asked teens: "If you could have a guaranteed great time, whom would you rather have it with, your family or your friends?"

The key phrase here is "guaranteed great time." Either way, we are assuring teens of a great experience. Of course, what teens do with friends when they have a "great time" may be quite

# Teens Want to Be With Their Friends

*Teens, by a margin of almost two to one, choose friends over family when asked with whom they would prefer to have a guaranteed great time.*

**(percent of teens citing family or friends as the group with whom they would prefer to have a guaranteed great time, by age, 1992)**

|  | family | friends |
|---|---|---|
| **Total teens** | **34%** | **64%** |
| Aged 12-15 | 40 | 58 |
| Aged 16-17 | 25 | 72 |
| Aged 18-19 | 35 | 64 |

Source: TRU *Teenage Marketing & Lifestyle Study*

different from what they imagine doing with their family. It's not surprising, then, that teens—by a margin of almost two to one—choose friends (63 percent) over family (35 percent). Although teens enjoy spending time with their family, if they have a better offer from friends, they'll leave their parents at the doorstep.

When we share these data with clients, those who are parents of teens nod their heads knowingly. They know they're lucky to get any quality time with their teenage children. They also know that the time they spend with their teens will be more enjoyable if their kids haven't turned down another offer to accept (begrudgingly) a family invitation.

For many parents, the hardest thing about raising a teenager is that their children's friends replace them early on as the most important people in their lives. Friends are the first people to whom teens turn with problems. They are the people with whom teens want to spend their free time.

Teens aged 16 and 17 have the strongest social ties to friends. These are the most rebellious years, with teens enjoying new freedoms: staying out later, partying, driving, and dating. The late motivational-research expert, Dr. Burleigh Gardner, described this mid-teen state as "the cutting of the apron string," the time when teens feel compelled to separate from family in almost every part of their lives.

The youngest teens are still somewhat under their parents' wings, which explains why so many say they would prefer to have a good time with their family. In contrast, high-school juniors and seniors will go out of their way to avoid spending leisure time with their parents. Recent graduates, however, often discover (and enjoy) their parents from a more adult perspective.

After making the initial choice of friends versus family, we asked respondents why they made this choice. The overriding

# Why Teens Would Rather Have a Great Time With Friends

*The overriding reason for those who chose friends was, "I can do things with my friends that there's no way I can do with my family."*

**(among teens who would prefer having a guaranteed great time with friends, percent citing selected reasons, 1992)**

|  | *percent* |
|---|---|
| I can do things with my friends that I can't do with my family. | 80% |
| I spend a lot of time at home with my family, so when I go out I want to be with friends. | 57 |
| I have more things in common with my friends than with my family. | 50 |
| My friends accept me as I am; they don't judge me. | 39 |
| I like my friends better than my family. | 13 |

Source: TRU *Teenage Marketing & Lifestyle Study*

# Why Teens Would Rather Have a Great Time With Family

*Those who chose to have a great time with their family say they appreciate the permanency of family in their lives.*

**(among teens who would prefer having a guaranteed great time with family, percent citing selected reasons, 1992)**

| | *percent* |
|---|---|
| Family will always be there, but friends can change | 69% |
| I don't get to spend enough time "having fun" with my family | 59 |
| The memories I'll have from a great time with my family will last longer | 52 |
| I like my family better than my friends | 25 |
| It's more unusual to have a great time with family | 18 |

Source: TRU *Teenage Marketing & Lifestyle Study*

reason for those who chose friends was, "I can do things with my friends that there's no way I can do with my family!"

"I wouldn't go out even with my brothers and sisters and let loose at a dance club like I could with my friends," said a 16-year-old girl.

"When we go to the movies, my friends and I look for the cute guys. I would never do that with my parents!" said a 15-year-old girl.

The other reasons teens give for choosing friends over family revolve around the theme of "I just wanna have fun (with my friends)." For example, 57 percent of teens say they prefer to be with friends because they already spend so much time with their family. These teens must be counting the time they spend at home sleeping, talking on the phone with friends, or hanging out behind the closed door of their room!

Those who chose to have a great time with their family responded maturely, saying they appreciate the permanency of family in their lives. Parents of these teens should feel particularly gratified by their responses.

"Families provide unconditional love, and that's something you can't sacrifice," said a 17-year-old girl.

"If you get into a fight with friends, that could be the end of that relationship. But if you fight with your family, it gets resolved and it works out," said a 16-year-old girl.

One of our all-time favorite responses to any of our syndicated questions comes from those who chose family over friends, explaining, "It's more unusual to have a great time with family!" These teens seem to say, "Hey, having fun with my parents would be pretty weird. Why not, it's only one night!"

In general, marketers should portray teens having fun with one another. But for family-targeted brands, it's safe to show teens enjoying their parents and other family members. Although the teen years are still full of typical angst and parent-child conflict, teens not only admire and seek advice from their parents, but many also treasure the moments they share.

Parents of younger children might find these data encouraging. These parents are always hearing people say, "Enjoy your children when they're young because when they're teenagers, it's all over!" These data suggest that they still might have something to look forward to.

## How Teens Describe Their Families

Most teens like being with their family, perhaps because the generation gap is narrower than it used to be. Teens most often name mom or dad as the person they most admire. Mom is one of the first people teens turn to if they need advice. And although most teens prefer social outings with friends, a significant minority actually prefer having fun with their family.

Because of these results, we asked teens in a recent study to describe their families. The results show that teens hold their families in high regard. About 70 percent of the responses were positive, while only 30 percent were negative. Further, of the ten listed characteristics, the five that received the most responses all were positive.

Despite what many adults fear, most teens not only look up to their parents but feel good about their families. Teens are more likely to characterize their families as happy than unhappy, as loving than abusive, as close than cold, as supportive than "at each other's throats," and as fun than tense.

# How Teens Describe Their Families

*Teens are more likely to characterize their families as happy than unhappy.*

**(percent of teens citing positive or negative characteristics about their families, 1993)**

| Positive | *percent* | Negative | *percent* |
|----------|-----------|----------|-----------|
| Happy | 68% | Tense | 20% |
| Loving | 63 | At each other's throats | 18 |
| Supportive | 63 | Unhappy | 12 |
| Fun | 54 | Cold | 6 |
| Close | 45 | Abusive | 4 |

# Teens Who Describe Their Family as "Fun"

*African-American teens are more likely than Hispanic or white teens to describe their families as "fun."*

**(percent of teens saying their family is "fun," by race, ethnicity, and age, 1993)**

| Race | *percent* | Age | *percent* |
|------|-----------|-----|-----------|
| Blacks | 63% | 12-15 | 61% |
| Whites | 54 | 16-17 | 49 |
| Hispanics | 49 | 18-19 | 45 |

Source: TRU *Teenage Marketing & Lifestyle Study*

Although all five negative responses ranked at the bottom of the list, most of the teens who wrote in alternative responses answered negatively (47 of 73, or nearly two-thirds).

There are few significant differences in family characteristics by gender, age, or race with one exception: the characteristic of "fun." African-American teens are more likely than Hispanic or white teens to describe their family as "fun." Younger teens are also more likely to say their families are "fun." Younger teens, who are less involved in dating and other independent activities than older teens, are more likely to enjoy family outings and activities than teens aged 16 or older:

Creating advertising and promotions that teens find personally relevant is the key to successfully communicating with and appealing to teens. Only by understanding the attitudes and motivations that are the essence of being teen can you begin to develop and communicate personal relevance.

*Chapter Ten*

*Teen Social Concerns*

Teenagers are more societally conscious today than at any time in the recent past. Specifically, they are aware of a greater variety of social issues. When we ask teens to name the causes they care most about, they cite a wide variety ranging from AIDS and teenage pregnancy to ozone damage, guns, gangs, education, and child abuse. To a great extent, the media—from network television to in-school news programming, from music videos to benefit concerts—fuel this increased awareness.

Companies can find it beneficial to link their images and brands with social causes in marketing to teenagers. Cause-related marketing creates good will. Your brand may benefit if consumers know that purchasing it contributes to a cause that is important to them. Benetton and Cross Colours have linked their brands with the issue of race relations, Girbaud has linked with peace, and many other companies have tied into the issues of AIDS or the environment.

To do this successfully, it's important to select the most compelling causes for the teen segment you're targeting. Because of teens' fickle nature and their attraction to whatever is newest, you must stay attuned to whatever teens consider to be the current "hot" issues, being careful to avoid controversial causes, such as abortion or partisan politics. You should also steer clear of issues being used by too many other marketers. Based on these guidelines, the issues with the most potential for cause-related teen marketing right now are violence/gangs, child abuse, education, and race relations.

It has become vogue among teenagers to affiliate with one or more causes. This is yet one more way teens seek belonging and acceptance. As sincere as some teens are in their cause-related concerns and activities, you should keep in mind that many teens use causes to help them carve out an identity.

Affiliation with causes appears to be starting at a younger age than ever before. My son, who is now 11, won first prize when he was a first-grader with his anti-drug poster carrying the message, "I don't think I'd be your friend if you took drugs." Early and positive association with a cause not only increases a teen's awareness of issues but also enhances his or her self-esteem. In fact, my son's best friend, also age 11, has adopted a 1960s style of dress and mannerisms. While my son says, "See you!" to his mother and me when he leaves for school in the morning, his friend typically utters, "Peace is groovy, man!" I don't know how deep his feelings for peace really are, but I would guess they're not terribly deep. Instead, my son's friend is identifying with a certain attitude or group, and this is attracting him to the cause.

For effective cause-related marketing, it's important to understand that there is often a gap between teen attitudes and behavior. Seventy-eight percent of teens say that eating healthy is "in," for example. But we found that these 78 percent of teens ate the same amount of junk food as the 22 percent of teens who did not regard eating healthy as "in."

Twice a year we formally sit down with teens to discuss social issues: which issues they are aware of, which they care about, and which they are actively involved in. We do this to gain an understanding of why teens in our quantitative study find some issues more relevant than others. Specifically, we ask respondents in our study to choose the three issues (from a list of 19) that are most important to them.

## Teens and the Issue of AIDS

The issue of most importance to the largest number of teenagers is AIDS. Nearly half of all teens (and two-thirds of African-

# Most Important Social Concerns of Teens

*The issue of most importance to the largest number of teenagers is AIDS.*

**(percent of teens citing issue as one of three most important, 1995)**

|  | percent |
|---|---|
| AIDS | 44% |
| Education | 40 |
| Child abuse | 28 |
| Race relations | 28 |
| Violence | 28 |
| Drinking & driving | 24 |
| Abortion | 22 |
| Drug abuse | 18 |
| Environment | 18 |
| Animal rights | 15 |
| Economy | 14 |
| Unplanned pregnancy | 14 |
| Homelessness | 13 |
| Women's rights | 10 |
| War | 11 |
| Threat of nuclear war | 8 |
| Suicide | 9 |
| Health care | 7 |
| Divorce | 6 |

Source: TRU *Teenage Marketing & Lifestyle Study*

American teens) name AIDS as one of the three issues about which they care the most. Teens know they are personally at risk of contracting AIDS, though their behavior lags far behind their awareness.

In our qualitative research, we find that as much as teens intellectually understand the importance of using condoms and the consequences of not using them, in actual practice teens often engage in unsafe sex. Teens have a variety of reasons and rationalizations for not practicing safe sex. As much as teens understand the risk of AIDS, they simply don't believe it will happen to them. "We teens think we're invincible," explained a 16-year-old girl.

The second most-common explanation for not using condoms is "heat of the moment." As one 17-year-old boy said, "When you're in the right situation, you're feeling things, not thinking things."

Compounding this problem is alcohol and drug use. When teens (or adults) are under the influence of alcohol or drugs, they do not think as clearly as they normally would. Many teens have told us that when they are drunk or stoned, they're more willing to have sex (especially girls) and less likely to use (or demand) a condom.

"There's a lot of pressure to do drugs, drink, and have sex." Said a 14-year-old girl, "If you don't do what the others do, you'll be left out. If you do this stuff, you might get AIDS."

Teen girls have told us they are embarrassed to buy condoms. Teens of both genders find going to the store, choosing (or asking) for condoms, and paying for them awkward, to say the least. Some retailers will not sell condoms to teens, saying they are underage (though these same clerks will sell them cigarettes). One thing most teens agree on is that condoms should be easily accessible. Even socially conservative teens do not think teen abstinence is a realistic goal for all teenagers. For marketers to fully understand teenagers, they must recognize—and never discount—the pervasive power of teen sexuality.

## Teens and the Issue of Education

After AIDS, education is the most important concern of teens. Our findings suggest that teens are not satisfied with the quality of their education. They think the nation's educational system faces profound problems. With so many schools facing budget cuts, which affect teachers, textbooks, equipment, facilities, and classroom sizes, it's little wonder that today's teens consider education a primary issue. More than half of African-American teens and about one-third of Hispanic and white teens name education as a top issue.

One of the first signs of the declining confidence of teens in the educational system is how teens talk about their teachers. Our focus-group research has shown that teens' anecdotes about their teachers have become increasingly negative over the past few years.

We have been tracking this decline in our quantitative study as well. On two separate measures, the data show that teens think less of teachers than in the recent past. Ten years ago, teens rated educators as top role models (after only parents). Today, educators barely make it onto the list of role models. Teens also say they rarely turn to teachers, guidance counselors, or coaches with problems if they need advice. They would rather go to friends, parents, or siblings.

## Teens and the Issue of Race Relations

Beginning about three years ago, race relations became a top teen concern, coinciding with the Rodney King trial and the riots in

Los Angeles. Minority teens are particularly likely to name race relations as one of the three issues about which they care the most.

Multi-culturalism is increasingly important in the 1990s, and today's young people are on the forefront of this trend. Many teens, even today, complain that their parents have racist views and sometimes prohibit them from socializing with peers of different ethnic backgrounds.

We discovered this after conducting informal research at Amundson High School in Chicago, located in the heart of the city's north side. Amundson is probably unique, at least in Chicago, because of its ethnic diversity. The school boasts 39 languages spoken by its students, who represent 49 nationalities. The Amundson students are proud of their diversity and also of the fact that students of various ethnic backgrounds get along so well. The students are united by their individual interests more than their ethnicity or nationality. Those involved in sports cluster together, as do those interested in theater or student government, regardless of race or ethnicity.

Many of these teens told us that their parents forbid them to date someone of a different ethnic background. Whether it's African-American parents not wanting their child to associate with a Vietnamese student, or white parents not wanting their child to date a Filipino, the students we spoke with were exasperated by this problem. One 16-year-old Puerto Rican girl confessed that her father said he would (literally) kill her if she ever dated an African American. The students were frustrated by these restrictions, particularly since the punishment for disobeying their parents could be severe—from being grounded to being ostracized by the family. These teens believe that their generation is much more enlightened about race relations than their parents' generation. Interestingly, most of these teenagers are the children of baby boomers, who once lodged similar complaints against their parents.

The fact that today's teens are so concerned about race relations should encourage companies to be "inclusive" in marketing communications directed at teens. When choosing talent, consider showing a diversity of ethnicities, or developing multiple executions for reaching the diversity of teens. Nintendo of America has developed multiple executions of its "Play It Loud" campaign, which has been successful in enhancing its image (i.e., making it "cooler") among teens. For this campaign, the company uses music as an aid in boosting its image. Understanding how fragmented teens' musical taste is these days, Nintendo and its advertising agency, Leo Burnett, created separate executions featuring grunge and hip hop. This sensitivity to teen diversity is not only politically smart, but also savvy marketing: it makes the advertising personally relevant to significantly more members of Nintendo's consumer base.

Thirty percent of American teens today are minorities. And the minority population is growing at a faster rate among teenagers than among adults. Even these numbers, though, understate the importance (and minimum risk) of being inclusive. Not only do many white teens go to school, recreate, and "hang" with minority peers, for example, but many of them also emulate minorities (especially urban African Americans). They take lifestyle cues from African-American teens and from African-American culture at large. Similarly, depending upon the ethnic makeup of a school or community, some white teens also follow trends set by other minorities. Therefore, it's to an advertiser's benefit to appropriately feature ethnically diverse talent in teen-directed communications.

## Teens and the Issues of Violence and Gangs

The issue of violence is growing the fastest in its importance to teens, according to our study. For urban teens in particular, many of whom live in literal war zones, gangs and violence are a part of daily life. Gangs and wanna-be gangbangers are not confined to the cities, however. Even upper-middle-class suburbs and small towns see gang violence increasing. As with the issue of race relations, significantly more minority teens than white teens name violence as one of their top three concerns.

Most adults associate gangs with minorities and boys. But gangs are not exclusively male nor exclusively made up of minorities. It's now becoming fashionable for girls to affiliate with gangs.

"We deal with gangs everyday," said a 14-year-old girl. "I worry about the little kids."

"Our school has more gangbangers than any other type," said a 15-year-old boy. "It's our school, our neighborhood, and part of our life."

"There's so much violence in my neighborhood and a lot of pressure to join gangs," said a 16-year-old boy. "Sometimes, my mom is so scared she won't let us hang out outside."

Recently, we were conducting focus groups among high school boys. The subject was relationships. In the warmup to the discussion, we asked the boys to introduce themselves and tell us about the "weirdest" way they had ever met a friend. One of the boys, after introducing himself, said the weirdest way he met a friend was when the guy shot him. Although the backroom observers found the answer unexpected and provocative, to say the least, the other members of the focus group seemed to take it almost matter-of-factly. The respondent didn't give us many details about the incident, except to say that the experience brought him and the other guy together and now they're close friends. His comments speak to the reality of the world in which many teens grow up, one of pervasive violence that threatens their personal safety. Today, many teens need friends not only for companionship but also for protection in the volatile environment in which they live. That this one young man befriended the person who shot him also speaks to the tolerance and open-mindedness of today's teens.

## Teens and the Issues of Abortion and Child Abuse

Abortion and child abuse are issues of special importance for girls. Abortion ranks third among girls, while child abuse ranks fourth, after AIDS and education. Like their parents, teens are on both sides of the abortion issue, and often passionately so.

"I think that taking away a woman's right to choose what she does with her own body is taking away the fundamental human right of privacy," said a 19-year-old girl. "I am not pro-abortion, but I do believe a woman (not men in Washington) is the best (and only) judge of what is best for her. The repeal of Roe vs. Wade, in my opinion, would be a step backward for this country."

It may surprise some adults to know that many teens are pro-life, mirroring the attitudes of their parents. A significant number of teens believe abortion to be an act against God, as do many adults, showing how deep-seated this attitude is. About half of teens say that religion is one of the most important parts of their lives.

"I think abortion is a serious issue, because by allowing people to have abortions we are altering the natural pattern of life and could possibly be killing a child that has the brain capacity to find a cure for AIDS or cancer or save this planet," said a 15-year-old boy.

Unlike the abortion issue, there's only one side to the issue of child abuse, which—along with violence—is one of the fastest-growing teen issues. Just a few years ago, child abuse trailed the environment, drug abuse, and drinking and driving as a teen issue. But as some celebrities have revealed their own history of childhood abuse, and as other celebrities have had child-abuse claims leveled against them, teens are paying more attention to the issue.

"Child abuse is a top concern to me because it negatively affects the welfare of future generations," commented a 16-year-old girl.

At the moment, child abuse is one of the most attractive issues for corporate tie-ins because it is nonpartisan and growing in importance to teens.

## Teens and the Issue of the Environment

Three issues are declining in importance among teens: the environment, drinking and driving, and drug abuse. Just a few years ago, these issues ranked two, three, and four among teens. Only 18 percent of teens currently name the environment as one of their top three concerns. The proportion of teens who say the environment is "in" has fallen from 84 percent in 1990 to 77 percent in 1994.

In focus groups, teens have told us that they are tired of being lectured to about the environment by educators, other adults, and peers. Teens tell us that they and their friends make fun of "the kids who push the environment down our throats." For an issue as personally relevant to teens as the environment to decline so much in popular concern is alarming. It shows that the

# Teen Environmental Activities

*Girls are more likely to take part in environmental activities than boys.*

**(percent of teens taking part in selected activities, by gender, 1992)**

|  | *boys* | *girls* |
|---|---|---|
| Recycle cans/bottles | 61% | 65% |
| Buy environmentally friendly products | 41 | 57 |
| Recycle newspapers | 33 | 41 |
| Took part in Earth Day activities | 16 | 25 |

Source: TRU *Teenage Marketing & Lifestyle Study*

pedantic handling of an issue can greatly lessen its attractiveness to teenagers.

Although the environment is not as big a concern as it was in the past, teens still believe environmental issues are important. The environment is relevant to teens because they are the world's future, and they are the ones who will benefit or suffer the most from today's environmental policies and actions.

"It's cool to say we don't inherit the earth from our parents, we borrow it from our children—because it's so important," said one 15-year-old girl. "And there's a lot we can do about it that's really very simple."

Teens, like adults, often act in ways that contradict their attitudes. A study of adults found that approximately 80 percent consider themselves environmentalists, but it's unlikely that 80 percent of adults regularly recycle, let alone are actively involved in protecting the environment. For teens and adults, it's easier to pay lip service to a cause than to actually get involved.

A larger proportion of teens are concerned about the environment than act on those concerns. Still, most teens regularly recycle cans, bottles, or newspapers. About half try to buy "green" products, and a fifth have participated in Earth Day activities. As with many issues, girls are more involved than boys. Girls are more likely to participate in all four of the pro-environment activities we covered in our study.

As one 16-year-old girl said, "I buy products that are better for the environment. If I'm at the store and I see two kinds of paper, and one says 'made from 100 percent recycled paper,' I'll buy that one."

Not only are teens concerned about the environment, they are also motivated to do something about it. It's likely that tomorrow's adults will demand more "green" products. Marketers who jump on the environmental bandwagon have a better chance of creating goodwill among teens than those who ignore environmental concerns. Still, don't bet that teens will pay more for your brand simply because it's environmentally friendly.

## Teens and the Issues of Drinking and Drugs

The issues of drinking and drugs have also fallen in importance to teens. Part of the blame lies in the advertising community itself. Although teens were hit hard with anti-drug and anti-drinking-and-driving messages, often the executions were laughable. Words like "no" and "don't" might work when you're talking to five- and six-year-olds. But teens find these reprimands and warnings preposterous. The best way to turn teens off is to preach to them. The best way to reach them is to show teens the consequences: make them feel the issue. Don't say, "Just say no." This Nancy Reagan slogan became a joke in almost every high school in the country.

Public service announcements don't have to preach. The recent ads from the Centers for Disease Control (CDC) promoting the use of condoms, for example, were a praiseworthy step in the right direction. Rather than being preachy, they were relevant. The 30-second dancing-condom commercial (in which a condom hops out of a drawer and into bed with a couple whose genders are not revealed) makes its point clearly and compellingly.

At a political fundraiser in Chicago a few years ago, I had the honor of meeting President Clinton. I was one of about 100 people who were to spend about 15 seconds with the president while a photographer took our picture shaking his hand. I went to this event with two friends, and the three of us discussed what we would say to the president in our allotted time. We were

# Teen Boys and Girls Differ on Issues

*Women's rights, abortion, and child abuse are more important issues to girls than to boys.*

**(issues with at least a ten percentage point difference in the percentage of males and females naming it as one of the three most important, percent citing by gender, 1995)**

|                 | boys | girls |
| --------------- | ---- | ----- |
| Abortion        | 17%  | 28%   |
| Child abuse     | 20   | 35    |
| Education       | 44   | 34    |
| War             | 16   | 6     |
| Women's rights  | 5    | 16    |

Source: TRU *Teenage Marketing & Lifestyle Study*

debating whether to offer profound words of wisdom (rather presumptive of us!) or keep the banter light. I opted to mention to the president that, for a living, I tested teens' reactions to advertising and that the CDC ads were among the most powerful I had seen. The president seemed particularly pleased, not only because I wasn't giving him advice but also because he seemed genuinely interested. In fact, my comments and his questions bought me at least twice as much time with the president as my friends—until I was pulled away by those whose job it is to keep the line moving!

The declining importance of the problems of drug abuse and drinking and driving among teens is also testament to teens' attraction to that which is newest. As new issues gain media attention, such as AIDS, gangs, and child abuse, older issues such as drunk driving or drug abuse take a backseat. To renew the importance of these issues to teens will require new campaigns and newsworthy events.

## Other Issues of Importance to Teens

Today's teenage boys seem to be enlightened about a few note-worthy issues, such as reproductive responsibility, indicating that as adults they may have a better understanding of these issues than today's adult men. More boys than girls, for example, name unplanned pregnancy as one of their top three social concerns. Additionally, 5 percent of boys name women's rights as a top-three concern. Considering that the boys could choose among 19 issues, 5 percent is a noteworthy number.

Sixteen percent of girls name women's rights as one of their three top issues, placing it 10th among the 19 issues we measured. The National Organization for Women, which is developing a program of high school chapters, is counting on this generation of young women to become actively involved in women's issues.

# Importance of Issues by Race and Ethnicity

*More than half of African-American and Hispanic teens are concerned about AIDS.*

**(five most important issues to teens, percent citing by race and ethnicity, 1995)**

|  | *percent* |
| --- | --- |
| **African Americans** | |
| AIDS | 61% |
| Education | 51 |
| Race relations | 37 |
| Violence | 37 |
| Child abuse | 23 |
| **Hispanics** | |
| AIDS | 54 |
| Education | 43 |
| Race Relations | 42 |
| Violence | 31 |
| Abortion | 17 |
| **Whites** | |
| AIDS | 39 |
| Education | 36 |
| Child abuse | 28 |
| Drinking and driving | 27 |
| Violence | 25 |

Source: TRU *Teenage Marketing & Lifestyle Study*

Teen girls are more concerned with issues they consider personally relevant, such as AIDS, education, race relations, violence, and the environment. It will be interesting to see if women's rights becomes a more important concern to teen girls after all the media attention on spousal abuse and sexual harassment.

Women's rights, abortion, and child abuse are more important issues to girls than to boys. Conversely, education, drug abuse, the economy, and war are more important to teen boys.

There are also racial differences in the issues of most importance to teens. While AIDS and education are the top two issues for all racial and ethnic groups, a larger share of African-American and Hispanic teens are concerned about these issues than white teens. Minority teens are also more likely to cite race relations and violence as important issues than are white teens. Race relations ranks third in importance among African-American and Hispanic teens but seventh among white teens (cited by only 23 percent). Violence ranks fourth among African-American and Hispanic teens but fifth among whites.

# Chapter Eleven
# Advertising to Teens

Much of the work we do at TRU is advertising research, and almost all of it is qualitative. This experience affords us a rich understanding of what advertising means to teenagers, how teens view and interact with advertising, and the type of advertising that is most effective with teens. Understanding how and why teens react the way they do to advertising is an evolving process. Though we get better at evaluating advertising from a teen perspective each year, we are still at times surprised by teens' reactions to marketing communications. What we learned from a recent advertising concept project for Keebler is an example of how surprising teens can be. The advertising concepts were created by Keebler's long-standing ad agency, Leo Burnett Co. We've been involved in several Keebler/Burnett advertising projects over the past few years, so we're well aware of the equity that the Keebler elves bring to the brand; they comfort moms and attract the attention and imagination of children. Still, we weren't sure what the reaction would be when I showed a Keebler advertising concept, with the elves pictured dancing around packages of chips, to a couple of 16-year-old boys. We were concerned that these older teens might slam the elves. To our (pleasant) surprise, the two boys (one who had the voice and attitude of Butt-Head of MTV fame) lit up when the elves appeared, even more than the second graders I had talked to an hour earlier! When I asked them what they thought of the end frame with the dancing elves, the Butt-Head guy said, "If it's a conga line, then that's cool!" (The suggested conga line appeared in a later execution.) The moral of this story: don't second-guess what teens will think is cool in advertising. Check it out!

It's important to recognize right from the start that teens view advertising differently than do adults. To teens, advertising is more than product information (but never forget the importance of providing teens with adequate product information). To teens, advertising is popular culture.

Just as teenagers discuss the latest episode of "Melrose Place," new movies, or new music videos, they also talk to one another about advertising. Sometimes they praise it. Other times, they trash it. Unlike most adults, teens are literally surrounded on a daily basis by hundreds, sometimes thousands, of peers with time on their hands. They spend some of this time discussing their favorite, and least favorite, commercials.

TRU has developed a quantitative measure that shows the importance of advertising to teens. Based on a series of agree/ disagree statements, this measure uncovers the degree of teens' involvement with advertising. The findings show that teens are highly involved, with older teens, girls, and African Americans the most involved with and entertained by advertising.

These data confirm that advertising is entertaining to teens, which explains why it is such a frequent topic of teen conversation. Eighty percent of teens agree that, "Sometimes my friends and I will talk about a commercial we either really like or hate." Significantly more older teens and girls than younger teens and boys agree with this statement. Significantly more African-American teens than white or Hispanic teens agree.

Being a topic of conversation is not necessarily a "positive" for an ad. Even if an ad is favorably discussed among teens, it still needs to be clear and persuasive enough to generate sales or shift attitudes. If an ad is received poorly by teens, the negative talk about it may tarnish the image of the brand and result in teen rejection of the product.

Many teens are extremely analytical when discussing advertising, while others react more simply and pointedly. As one

# Teens Talk
# About Commercials

*Advertising is entertaining to teens, which explains why it is such a frequent topic of teen conversation.*

**(percent of teens agreeing strongly/somewhat with the statement, "Sometimes my friends and I will talk about a commercial we either like or hate," by gender, age, race, and ethnicity, 1994)**

|  | *percent* |
|---|---|
| **Total** | **80%** |
| Boys | 76 |
| Girls | 84 |
| Aged 12 to 15 | 77 |
| Aged 16 to 17 | 82 |
| Aged 18 to 19 | 83 |
| White | 81 |
| African-American | 86 |
| Hispanic | 80 |

Source: TRU *Teenage Marketing & Lifestyle Study*

15-year-old girl said, "Advertising that's interesting to watch and makes a statement is the type that catches my attention and might later influence me to buy something."

Equally opinionated is the 16-year-old boy who commented, "Bad commercials are the ones that are dumb or suck."

Teens want advertising to be entertaining. In fact, three-fourths agree that, "Good advertising can be really entertaining." Surprisingly, the oldest teens are most likely to say they are entertained by advertising, evidence that this feeling is not just youthful enthusiasm.

Two-thirds of teens agree that, "Good advertising helps me make decisions about what to buy," and slightly fewer agree that, "Good advertising can make me think or feel better about a product or company."

Although entertaining ads can generate interest in a product, teenagers also take cues from other information sources. Nevertheless, the fact that a sizable majority of teens at least somewhat agree that advertising helps in purchase decisions shows that most teens recognize advertising's importance to them as consumers. This finding is confirmed by other measures in our syndicated study. When we ask teens, "What makes a brand cool?" many name advertising. Similarly, when we ask them where they find out about the latest trends, advertising ranks high.

Teens hold high standards for advertising because they've enjoyed so many specific ads. Most teens think that advertisers are not meeting these standards. Only about two-fifths agree with the statement, "I think advertisers do a good job creating advertising for people my age." With so many brand choices available to consumers, creating compelling and memorable

# Teen Attitudes Toward Advertising

*Three-fourths of teens agree that, "Good advertising can be really entertaining."*

**(percent of teens agreeing strongly/somewhat with selected statements, 1994)**

| | percent who agree | | |
|---|---|---|---|
| | total agree | strongly agree | somewhat agree |
| Good advertising can be really entertaining. | 75% | 37% | 38% |
| Good advertising helps me make decisions about what to buy. | 66 | 27 | 39 |
| Good advertising can make me think or feel better about a product or company. | 63 | 26 | 37 |
| Bad advertising can make me think or feel worse about a product or company. | 61 | 34 | 27 |
| Advertisers do a good job in creating ads for people my age. | 44 | 14 | 30 |

Source: TRU *Teenage Marketing & Lifestyle Study*

advertising is more important than ever. Because teens can tune out a brand simply because of bad advertising, the stakes for marketers are dramatically high. More than 60 percent of teens agree that, "Bad advertising can make me think or feel worse about a product or company."

Understanding the risks of exposing teens to advertising that is less than honest, mediocre, or confusing underscores how critical it is to get it right the first time. By following teens' "rules for advertisers," you can greatly increase the odds of developing ads that teens embrace rather than reject. Just as teens can be a most unforgiving audience, they can also be the most embracing.

## The Rules of Advertising, According to Teens

To marketers, advertising creates awareness, provides product information, communicates a brand's image, and hopefully persuades consumers to try (or continue to use) a brand. To teens, advertising is a means of collecting product information, and it is a form of entertainment.

Teens are often skeptical about advertising, quick to reject ads they feel are off target. Because teens are highly segmented demographically and psychographically, different approaches work better with different teen audiences. The challenge for marketers is to create compelling and entertaining advertising that not only attracts most teens, but also does not alienate any single teen segment. Certainly, advertising that is inclusive, representing the diversity of today's U.S. teenage population, will reach the broadest audience.

In our syndicated study, we ask teenagers to list the do's and don'ts of creating effective teen-directed advertising. We developed this measure by first testing it qualitatively, talking to teens in-depth about advertising in a number of different markets. We showed teens a variety of teen-directed commercials, some that we thought were excellent and others poor. After showing them the ads, we got them talking and jotted down their thoughts on an easel pad while we talked. The teens were so involved in the discussion that we literally papered the room with sheets from the easel pad in market after market! We combined, condensed, and modified the rules, creating a list that we quantified in our syndicated study.

Specifically, we asked our national sample of teens: "Which of the following do you think are the most important rules companies should follow when advertising to teens?" Teens could check up to 5 of the 26 rules.

## Rule One: Be Funny

Four of the top five rules have remained constant over the two years that we have tracked this question. One constant is, "be funny."

Nothing attracts teens to advertising more than humor. Whenever we ask teens to name their favorite commercials, they inevitably list those that employ humor. Humor is effective because, if done right, it can have nearly universal teen appeal. Other executional elements, such as celebrities or music, may not appeal to all teens and could alienate some. But humor can appeal to almost all, and it can be combined with other executional elements to create a synergistic effect. A celebrity can be shown using an advertised product in a humorous way, for example.

Humor, however, is not the answer to every advertising strategy. In fact, humor can be counterproductive in communicating certain strategies. Selling a new, high-tech product, for example, may be better done without humor. Reebok's original

# Rules for Advertisers

*Nothing attracts teens to advertising more than humor.*

**(percent of teens selecting statement as one of top five
rules for advertisers, by gender, 1994)**

|  | *total* | *boys* | *girls* |
|---|---|---|---|
| Use humor/be funny | 60% | 62% | 57% |
| Be honest | 55 | 54 | 57 |
| Be clear with message | 45 | 44 | 47 |
| Be original | 38 | 36 | 41 |
| Don't try too hard to be "cool" | 37 | 38 | 36 |
| Use great music that fits | 34 | 35 | 33 |
| Don't use sex to sell | 33 | 25 | 41 |
| Make ads teens can relate to | 33 | 29 | 37 |
| Grab attention right away | 30 | 31 | 28 |
| Show/demonstrate product | 29 | 31 | 28 |
| Don't preach | 29 | 27 | 30 |
| Show things/people realistically | 29 | 25 | 33 |
| Don't talk down to teens | 27 | 26 | 28 |
| Make ads for teens, not parents | 23 | 24 | 22 |
| Don't butcher a good song | 21 | 24 | 18 |
| Be politically correct | 20 | 19 | 21 |
| Don't try to be "teen" | 19 | 19 | 19 |
| Show sexy girls | 19 | 34 | 3 |
| Use current teen slang | 14 | 14 | 15 |
| Use new, different celebrities | 13 | 13 | 14 |
| Show teens or those slightly older | 13 | 13 | 13 |
| Use celebs who fit the product | 12 | 12 | 11 |
| Don't be obvious you're selling something | 12 | 12 | 12 |
| Show sexy guys | 9 | 5 | 13 |
| Use fantasy | 8 | 10 | 6 |
| Tell who the advertiser is right away | 7 | 8 | 6 |

Source: TRU *Teenage Marketing & Lifestyle Study*

advertising for its Pump shoe humorously depicted coach Pat Riley and a few basketball players bent down on the basketball floor pumping their Reeboks. But teen athletes take their shoes seriously. They told us they were unsure of the technological soundness of Pumps; their doubts seemed to come from the humorous tone of the commercials.

Reebok's advertising for its next generation of Pumps, the InstaPump, was serious and more "next generation" in tone. It showed the evolution of pump technology. When we tested this campaign among high-school athletes, the teens believed in the technology and appreciated the serious and compelling way Reebok presented this high-ticket item to them. They believed the shoes would fit tighter to provide stronger ankle support, which would result in increased performance; they would be able to run faster and jump higher.

## Rule Two: Be Honest

After humor, teens most appreciate honesty in advertising. In fact, they demand it. As anyone who has any contact with teens knows, teenagers are cynical. If they detect a less-than-honest (or less-than-believable) advertising claim, they may reject the product or brand. To teens, exaggeration can seem dishonest, even if done in jest. Remember, teens are extremely savvy about advertising. Hype or insincerity quickly turns them off. If what you're telling them is based on fantasy, be clear that you're asking them to suspend their disbelief. Teens can be extremely literal and reject anything they don't find believable.

More than adults, teens find out about products and advertising from their peers. Word-of-mouth about a dishonest or "dumb" ad can spread like wildfire in teen circles. As one 18-year-old boy said, "I hate it when advertising says one thing but does something else. When we find out the truth, it just makes us mad."

Recently, Sprite has been running a campaign we originally tested in storyboard form. The essence of the campaign, known as "Obey Your Thirst," is honesty. One of the executions, titled "What is Cool?," directly attacks the teen obsession with coolness. It shows a teen obsessing over whether everything he does is cool (with the emphasis on the assumption that everything he does is cool), including what he drinks. Another execution entitled, "What They Will Tell You," confronts the gratuitous use of celebrities and hype to sell products. The spots end with the lines, "Image is Nothing. Thirst is Everything. Obey Your Thirst. Sprite." Teens found this approach refreshing, a product attribute (not incidentally) the advertiser had hoped to communicate.

## Rule Three: Be Clear

This rule probably overlaps the "be honest" rule. In fact, 67 percent of teens warn advertisers to "be honest" or "be clear."

Many media directors, when presented and struggling with an ad to place that doesn't really communicate its message as immediately as it should, convince themselves (and sometimes their unwitting clients) that teens eventually will get the message through repeated exposures. But when exposed to a confusing ad teens may say, "Yeah, that was cool. But what did it mean?" The point is, teens want to get the message, and they want to get it right away.

Advertisers should remember that there are too many alternatives available at the push of a button to expect teens to sit through an ad again and again until the message sinks in, no matter how cool or funny the execution. As important as it is to entertain, clear communication can never take a backseat.

## Rule Four: Be Original

As with most of the top rules, this is one with which both teens and advertisers agree. Advertisers know they need to set their brands and messages apart from others. Teens appreciate those rare ads that do so, that are compelling, entertaining, or provocative in an original way. When we hear teens say, "Wow, that's different! I've never really seen a commercial like that before," we know our client is really onto something (assuming, of course, it's communicating as intended). Originality is especially important in ads for which humor would be strategically off track. If you're not going to leave them laughing, leave them thinking or feeling. Work to get teens' attention quickly; their attention span is short. Then, hold their attention throughout the 30 or 60 seconds.

When testing advertising concepts, always ask: Does the idea communicate its intended message? Is the message important and believable? Is the concept age appropriate? Can teens (or the teen target) personally relate to the idea and its execution? And, is the premise new or different? If an advertising concept fails any of these key tests, an advertiser should either change it appropriately or abandon it altogether.

## Rule Five: Don't Try too Hard to Be Cool

We included this rule in the list in our quantitative study because of the many times we've heard teens say, after watching a commercial, "Some adult came up with that one just trying to sound cool!"

Don't underestimate teenagers. They're incredibly perceptive and draw the line when they feel a copywriter is pushing the coolness button too far. The problem lies in the difference between what the copywriter thinks is "cool" to teens and what teens consider "cool." It's better to incorporate "cool" elements only if they enhance the message. Don't try to be cool for the sake of being cool. It almost always backfires.

## Use Great Music That Fits

The problem with teens' short attention span is made worse by advertising clutter. Again, don't count on teens to be patient or to persevere in trying to get your message. Still, there is a device that will get teens to watch your ad over and over again: great music.

Not only is music inherently appealing and compelling to teens, it offers two tactical advantages when used appropriately in advertising. First, if teens like a tune or song in an ad, they undoubtedly will pay more attention to the ad. Second, music can signal to teens that an ad is for them. If an ad features a hip-hop, alternative, or metal soundtrack or song, teens know it's for them, and teens crave ownership.

When choosing music for an ad, don't automatically use whatever is the latest and greatest. A catchy original tune, when supported by relevant messages and compelling visuals, can be timeless.

Steer clear of specific musical acts because their popularity among teenagers will probably be short-lived. It's safer to use a style of music that is popular, although there are exceptions. One of our favorite ads is a Nike execution from a few years back known as "Instant Karma," featuring the John Lennon song of the same name. When we tested the commercial in focus groups of urban teens, they liked the spot and the song (which plays throughout and comprises the entire audio track), though only a few teens could identify the artist (and even then they named the Beatles rather than solo Lennon). "It's some '60s song, but it's cool and I like it," said one respondent. Nike happened to choose a song which transcends the generation from which it arose. The song worked because it was appropriate for the execution. Remember, the rule is to use great music that *fits*.

Many adults regard Beatles songs and other music from the 1960s as sacred, disdaining their commercial use. But the only way to expose teens en masse to this great music may be to use it in commercials. My brother Paul, who supports his songwriter/singer career by also working as a music journalist, once asked Yoko Ono during an interview what she thought of Nike using her late husband's music. She was thrilled the music was reaching today's younger generation, regardless of the medium, she told him.

Coke's current "Always Coca-Cola" campaign is another example of advertising music that teens love (particularly girls), though stylistically the original tune did not necessarily fit with current teen tastes. (Since then, Coke has wisely made the tune more inclusive to appeal to a more diverse audience, airing R&B and "world music" versions.) We recently conducted a series of immersion events entitled "Wise Up to Teens!" to open marketers' eyes, ears, and even taste buds to teenage America. In one segment, we presented a video edited from tape shot by a group of teens to show their daily lives. One of the questions asked of teens by the teen interviewer was, "What's your favorite commercial?" Girl after girl mentioned the Coke tune, with three girls singing it in unison on the video.

It's safer to use a genre of music rather than a specific artist, and it can also be more compelling. Similarly, it's safer to use original music. Whatever you do, as teens admonish, don't butcher good music (rule 15). Levi's "Got to Be Real" campaign for its 501 brand featured a song of the same name. When discussing this campaign in focus groups, teens told us that the song was what they best liked in the spot. One boy actually stood up in a focus group and sang the song, accompanying himself on air guitar!

## Show and Demonstrate the Product

It may be surprising that so many teens advise advertisers to demonstrate their product. Showing a product sounds mundane and unteen-like. But teens, like adults, expect advertising to provide product information. Teens can get frustrated and tune out advertising that doesn't answer basic product questions.

In our long list of rules for advertisers, a rule called "Show and demonstrate the product" probably sounds less than exciting to teens. If instead we had called the rule, "Tell me what I need to know about your product," it's likely that more teens would have chosen it as one of their top five. Still, enough chose it even in its current state to indicate just how important conveying a relevant product message is to teens.

Product as "star" is probably more important in the videogame category than in others we regularly research. TRU has conducted much of Nintendo's qualitative copy research over the past few years, working with its advertising agency, Leo Burnett. We've also done qualitative research for Konami, one of the largest makers of videogames for Nintendo and Sega. No matter how much of a television spot is devoted to showing product shots, we find that teens want more. Of course, simply showing game footage isn't enough. That alone cannot communicate brand imagery or fully engage teens in a commercial. But in the case of the videogame category, product shots are often the heart of the commercial. How the product is shown and framed (along with the game action itself, of course) are what set each execution apart.

## Don't Preach, Don't Talk Down to Teens

These two rules rank high in the list. Fifty-six percent of teens name one or the other as one of the five most important rules for advertisers. We added "don't preach" to the list last year. Before we did this, "don't talk down to teens" was the number-five rule, underscoring the importance of this guideline.

If there were a short list of essential rules that must be heeded in any successful teen-directed advertising, "don't talk down" would be on it (along with "be honest," "be clear" and either "be funny" or "be original"). Teens will reject advertising that they find patronizing.

Remember, teens have a different idea of what is condescending than do middle-aged executives. At the very least, run your copy by a group of teens for a disaster check (not a surprising recommendation from a researcher!). Empathize with teens. Show you understand what's important to them without being condescending. Like adults, teens need to feel respected.

## Don't Use Teen Slang

Lately, there has been a proliferation of advertising that uses teen slang. Marketers use teen slang in an attempt to create ads that signal to teens that a product is for them, but "teenspeak" usually backfires. If teens feel that an advertiser is trying too hard to be teen, they may reject the advertising as condescending.

In focus groups, we've asked teens about the issue of teen slang in advertising. In a recent project, each group consisted of three sets of buddy pairs, each pair representing one school. When we first asked respondents if they thought advertisers should use slang in advertising, most were enthusiastic about the idea. Then we asked each pair to list some of the newest words in use around their school. Although the six teens were from the same general area, they were unfamiliar with several of the words named by their fellow respondents. What's "in" at one school may not be in at a school across town. After this exercise, the respondents (without prompt from the moderator) recanted their earlier advice, saying, "Well, on second thought, maybe advertisers should not use slang!"

Marketers should avoid using all but the most basic slang (e.g., "cool," "sucks, "man") in advertising for a variety reasons:

• Teens want their private language to remain private. They don't want adults to understand or to use "teenspeak."

• Slang words are interpreted differently by different teens depending on where they live, their ethnicity, and so on.

• Not all words appeal to all teen demographic segments.

• Language is perhaps the most volatile aspect of teen lifestyle; new words are constantly entering the teen vernacular and old words discarded.

• Slang is extremely faddish and short-lived. What may be "in" at the time of production may very well be "out" by the time an ad hits the air. Slang is not essential in creating relevant teen advertising. Instead, look to music, fashion, and appropriate talent, which are all less risky means of achieving the same objective.

## Sex in Advertising

Most teens agree about the top five rules in advertising, but there is less consensus about others. Not surprisingly, there is little agreement regarding the use of sex in advertising.

One-third of teens select "don't use sex to sell" as one of the their top five rules for advertisers. Notably, this advice is offered by 41 percent of girls but only 25 percent of boys.

When teenage boys are asked what they most want to see in advertising, they quickly answer, "girls" (although their vernacular reveals more about what they're actually looking for here). When teenage girls are asked what they think about sex in advertising, a typical response is the one we got from a 16-year-old: "If it's relevant to what they're selling, like condoms, then it's OK." Only 13 percent of girls chose "show sexy guys" as one of their top five rules for advertisers.

Girls want a reason for using sex in advertising. Boys, on the other hand, don't need to see a connection. They just want to see girls, and the sexier, the better. One in three boys named "show sexy girls" as one of their top five rules for advertisers. If your target is females only, or males and females, be extremely cautious about using sex in advertising. The more sensitive your communication in this area, the safer it will be.

## The Personal Relevance Rules

The bottom line in creating effective teen advertising is to establish personal relevance. Teens need to see themselves in an ad, either based on their own self-image or their aspired image, to grasp right away that it is for them. By following the four rules listed below (ranked sixth, eighth, twelfth, and fourteenth), advertisers can create personal relevance for teens.

# The Personal Relevance Rules

*Teens need to see themselves in an ad, either based on their own self-image or their aspired image, to grasp right away that an ad is for them.*

**(percent of teens citing statement as one of top five rules for advertisers, 1994)**

|  | *percent* |
|---|---|
| Use great music that fits | 34% |
| Make ads teens can relate to | 33 |
| Show things/people realistically | 29 |
| Make ads for teens, not parents | 23 |
| Teens citing at least one of these statements | 70 |

Source: TRU *Teenage Marketing & Lifestyle Study*

Overall, 70 percent of teens cite at least one of these rules among their top five. The most effective teen advertising, then, communicates to teens clearly and honestly. It signals that a product is for them, and it does so in an entertaining and compelling way.

## Preferred Advertising Settings

An important executional decision is the setting for teen advertising. In one of our recent syndicated studies, we asked teens to choose the one setting (from a list of eight) that they most like to see in advertising. The top answer was beaches. To teens, there's no setting that communicates fun more than the beach. Going to the beach is one of the most popular and stable teen activities. Even when we combine responses for forests and mountains, the beach is still by far the most preferred advertising setting.

Girls are the biggest beach fans, with more than twice as many selecting beaches as their preferred setting over their second-most popular response, American cities. Although the beach is also boys' favorite setting, significantly fewer boys than girls select this response.

American cities also hold appeal for teens. Not surprisingly, significantly more urban and suburban teens than rural teens select American cities as one of their favorite settings. More than twice as many African Americans (35 percent) than whites (16 percent) select cities. About 25 percent of Hispanic teens also choose American cities.

## The Rules for Consumer Promotions

Although this chapter is devoted to advertising, a discussion of teen-directed promotions seems appropriate for two reasons. First, in these days of integrated marketing, there is greater

# Teens Prefer Certain Advertising Settings

*The beach is the number-one setting
teens like to see in ads.*

**(percent of teens saying they prefer site as a setting for ads,
by gender, 1994)**

|                   | total | boys | girls |
|-------------------|-------|------|-------|
| Beaches           | 37%   | 30%  | 44%   |
| American cities   | 20    | 23   | 17    |
| Forests           | 16    | 19   | 12    |
| Rugged mountains  | 11    | 13   | 8     |
| Farmland          | 7     | 7    | 7     |
| Green hills       | 7     | 7    | 7     |
| Foreign cities    | 5     | 4    | 6     |
| Deserts           | 1     | 1    | 1     |

Source: TRU *Teenage Marketing & Lifestyle Study*

# Teen Participation in Promotions

*The two most popular promotions among teens
are free samples and coupons.*

**(percent of teens participating in selected types of consumer promotions during the past 30 days, by gender and age, 1994)**

|  | | gender | | age | | |
| --- | --- | --- | --- | --- | --- | --- |
|  | *total* | *boys* | *girls* | *12-15* | *16-17* | *18-19* |
| Free sample | 45% | 39% | 51% | 48% | 47% | 38% |
| Coupon | 38 | 32 | 44 | 35 | 40 | 42 |
| Contest/sweepstakes | 23 | 23 | 23 | 26 | 21 | 19 |
| Free gift with purchase | 23 | 20 | 26 | 25 | 21 | 20 |
| Cash rebate | 11 | 12 | 10 | 11 | 10 | 11 |
| Frequent-buyer clubs | 7 | 8 | 6 | 6 | 8 | 9 |

Source: TRU *Teenage Marketing & Lifestyle Study*

awareness that linking advertising and promotion campaigns adds to the cohesiveness and effectiveness of your message. Second, almost all of the rules for advertising to teens also apply when promoting to teens.

In our syndicated study, we ask teens which of six types of consumer promotions they participated in during the past 30 days. The results show that most teens participate in consumer promotions that offer immediate gratification. The two most popular promotions among teens are free samples (45 percent participate) and coupons (38 percent). Contests/sweepstakes (23 percent), free gift with purchase (23 percent), cash rebates (11 percent), and frequent-buyer clubs (7 percent) follow.

More girls than boys take advantage of free samples and coupons, probably because girls do more shopping than boys. More younger than older teens participate in sampling and contests, while the oldest teens prefer coupons.

During the past several years, TRU has been involved in evaluating a range of potential teen-targeted promotions, from in-school sampling to major-event marketing. A common thread runs through those that were most successful: they were simple. Teens respond most to promotions in which they can easily participate. Promotions that take too much time, require too much effort, or involve chance are much less likely to engage teens. Still, if your objectives are to create brand awareness or to enhance imagery, the right contest, for example, can work regardless of low participation levels. Focus on your gain among those exposed to the promotion rather than on how many actually participate. Above all, keep your promotion easy, fun, and exciting, while offering an accessible reward.

*Chapter Twelve*

*How to Research Teens*

As a researcher, it's probably no surprise that I feel it appropriate and important to discuss how to research teens. Too often, teen research is done incorrectly. This chapter is a guide to the perils and pitfalls of teen research.

Research is an integral component of the marketing process, and it is particularly important in marketing to teens. Though you were once a teenager yourself, the older you are the more suspect your ability to predict how teens will react to a marketing concept. Despite our years of researching teens, we continue at times to be surprised by our findings.

Often, clients call and ask for an off-the-cuff evaluation of a marketing idea. When we suggest that they research teens' response rather than rely on our guess of how teens might react, they often say their schedule (or budget) doesn't allow it, that they're comfortable moving ahead on our recommendation. While our batting average in predicting teen reactions probably rises each year, we do not advise clients to proceed with a new piece of advertising or product idea without first checking it out with the target.

Several times, after concluding a presentation at a client's office, we've been asked to evaluate a new advertisement on the spot. This typically takes place in front of an audience that includes the account and strategic people from the agency who developed the strategy, the creatives who executed the strategy, and the client who approved the creative. Although we never say "no" to this invitation, we always preface our remarks by explaining how, despite spending the better part of each week talking to teens or analyzing their reactions to marketing ideas, we still find teens unpredictable. That's why we do research.

With that as a preface, this chapter explains how to do teen research, with special emphasis on qualitative analysis.

## First, Set the Objective

Each research project should begin with clear, realistic objectives. As basic as this may sound, some clients ask us to do research without a specific objective. For other clients, the objective sometimes boils down to nothing more than "we want to do research" or, "we thought we should do some focus groups." In fact, a highly worthwhile objective is to have brand managers and agency creatives simply listen to (and observe) consumers talking about the brand. The spark of an idea or the grasp of a consumer insight often comes when creatives personally attend focus groups. Unfortunately, creatives do not attend as much research as they should.

Most clients, though, come to us with specific objectives. More often than not, they describe their objectives over the telephone. Once in a while, we receive a formal Request for Proposal in which the objective for the proposed research is communicated in writing. As with copy strategy, research objectives that are committed to paper are typically well thought out. Writing down the objectives helps bring discipline to this critical stage of the process, making it easier to evaluate whether the objectives are achievable before beginning a project. The objectives should set the direction for your project, focusing on what needs to be and can be accomplished. The objectives determine whether the research should be qualitative (talking to teenagers in depth individually or in small groups), quantitative (asking teens to respond to a survey), or a combination of the two.

### Qualitative versus Quantitative

If your objectives begin with words like "explore," "probe," "develop hypotheses," "gain an understanding," or "brainstorm," then your research should be qualitative rather than quantitative. Qualitative research is open-ended and exploratory. It answers the "why's," providing a depth and richness of response.

If your research objectives begin with words such as "how many," "to determine," "to specify," "to test," and so on, quantitative research is probably what's called for. While qualitative research develops hypotheses, quantitative tests them. Qualitative gauges reactions, while quantitative determines the frequency of reactions among teen segments. Qualitative brainstorms for ideas, while quantitative measures the appeal of those ideas. Qualitative directs, while quantitative specifies.

Qualitative research is more flexible than quantitative research. While quantitative research is based upon a set questionnaire, qualitative research can change in midstream, especially when done by a skilled moderator. When researching teens, flexibility is a valuable tool.

Qualitative research is especially useful when your objective is to enhance, modify, or improve an idea. That's true whether the idea is a new product, a positioning or concept, or advertising. Teens are adept at understanding, reacting to, and offering ideas for improving concepts.

Qualitative research also reveals things that quantitative research cannot. It allows you to see teens' nonverbal reactions to ideas. It allows group synergy to emerge, which can be critically important in helping you develop or refine ideas. It allows you to probe responses as frequently and deeply as the subject matter or the respondents allow.

Observing nonverbal reactions is particularly important when researching teens, who often hide their real feelings. The importance of nonverbal response was brought home when we tested teen reactions to "warning labels" on RC Cola's teen-targeted Kick citrus soft-drink brand. Although the labels were designed to appear authentic, the actual copy reveals that they are in jest. The two we tested read: "Warning: This product will cause extreme stimulation of the taste buds and will send tremors of satisfaction to your brain," and "Warning: Kick: the hard-core, psycho drink in a bottle."

At an eight-person focus group, I passed around bottles of Kick with warning labels, asking the teens not to comment about the bottles aloud at first. By their immediate nonverbal reactions, we saw right away that the teens were intrigued by the labels and quickly got the joke, which they enjoyed. But during the in-depth discussion that followed, the teens became overly analytical about the choice of words used in the labels. Their verbal response was less enthusiastic. The nonverbal reactions, however, clearly showed us that the labels achieved their objective, creating immediate interest, curiosity, appeal, and age relevance.

## Qualitative Research Among Teens

Although the backbone of our company is our quantitative, syndicated *Teenage Marketing & Lifestyle Study*, the majority of our custom work is qualitative. In fact, as we've often remarked to clients, our syndicated study is probably the most "qualitative" quantitative study that exists as it includes everything from exploratory questions to respondent verbatims.

Two primary benefits of qualitative research are directness and flexibility: the ability to get in-depth reactions from consumers with the opportunity to probe and clarify immediately. If you are a first-time youth marketer, just seeing and hearing teenagers can be an eye-opening experience. Your first decision is which qualitative method to use. The three types of qualitative designs we use most often are one-on-ones (in-depth interviews with a single respondent), buddy pairs or dyads (interviews with two friends), and focus groups. We also use combinations, depending upon the objectives of the particular project. Your project's objectives should drive the design. While all three of the qualitative designs allow you to gain in-depth information, each has its own strengths and weaknesses, as outlined below.

## Teen Focus Groups

**Interaction.** Allows synergies among teens to spark new thoughts, ideas, and insights.

**Subject Matter.** Use when subject matter is such that teens will be unlikely to withhold information or temper remarks.

**Information.** Assumes most respondents can say all they need to say about a topic (unaided) in about 8 to 12 minutes in a full focus group or 15 to 20 minutes in a minigroup.

**Timing.** Relatively quick turnaround, depending upon eligibility incidence (the percent of the population that qualifies to participate in the research) and number of groups.

**Cost.** Relatively inexpensive on a cost-per-interview basis. Typically $3,500-$4,500 for a full (8 to 10 respondents) focus group and somewhat less for minigroups (4 to 6 respondents). The total cost will depend upon the number of groups, eligibility incidence, and the type of reporting and analysis required.

## Teen One-On-Ones

**Interaction.** Most effective when interaction among peers would be inhibiting or counterproductive to a project's objectives.

**Subject Matter.** Especially appropriate when the subject matter is particularly sensitive and teens might not want to talk about it in a group setting. Also appropriate if your research objective is to gauge how well a tested copy/concept/positioning communicates to teens.

**Information.** Allows greater depth of response. Effective when subject matter is complex or the information needed from an individual will require 20 to 30 minutes.

**Timing.** Depending upon the number of interviews involved for your project, more time may be required than for focus groups.

**Cost.** Typically, a higher cost per interview than for focus groups.

## Teen Buddy Pairs

**Interaction.** Particularly suited for products that are used by two people (e.g., a board game or videogame). Also effective for communication testing if done cautiously and properly. Can heighten comfort level of young respondents to encourage dialogue.

**Subject Matter.** This extremely flexible configuration can handle almost any subject matter.

**Information.** Allows for great depth of response.

**Logistics.** Sometimes difficult to recruit teens from low-incidence groups, since both friends need to qualify independently.

**Timing.** Similar to one-on-ones, timing can be longer than that for groups.

**Cost.** Between that of groups and one-on-ones on cost-per-respondent basis.

## Parent/Teen Pairs

**Interaction.** To gain insight into the purchaser/influencer or gatekeeper/initiator dynamic between parents and teens.

**Subject Matter.** Appropriate when the tested product is one that the parent purchases or "gatekeeps" but the teen is the predominant influencer or user (e.g., contact lenses, the family computer, a vacation, a family pet).

**Information.** Allows for in-depth understanding of both teens' and parents' perspectives on an issue, with the opportunity to confront them about any conflicts or inconsistencies in their perceptions.

**Logistics.** Research needs to be scheduled around parents' and teens' schedules.

**Cost.** As with friend pairs, cost per respondent is less than that of one-on-ones but higher than that of groups.

Qualitative research can go beyond these traditional designs. We sometimes use observational research (observing teens at venues where they congregate or use/purchase a product) because it offers unique insights. To paraphrase Yogi Berra, "You can observe a whole lot just by watching." We use observational research to gauge people's attraction to a product or service, how they interact with it, and the dynamics involved in using it or deciding to use it. We also use observational research for answering, "What's new?" or "What's the latest trend?"

Our Kids Research Unlimited division handles much of the qualitative research for Discovery Zone, which is the nation's leading chain of indoor playgrounds. To keep its FunCenters fresh and interesting to kids, Discovery Zone continually experiments with new additions. Rather than just talking to kids who have experienced these innovations, we observe them in the natural play environment. It's not hard to tell whether kids are having fun when they play. Additionally, our observational research allows us to see the sequence of play, how children interact with other kids in the environment, and how they allocate time between attractions.

We've also tested board games for Parker Brothers through observational research. This works best when the moderator explains the game's rules and gets the players going, then leaves the room during play and observes behind a one-way mirror.

In-store observational research can uncover the parent-teen dynamics of purchase influence, offering ideas for positioning. Observing how teens request items and how parents react to their requests can be enlightening. We've witnessed everything from out-and-out fights between parent and teen to teens sneaking items into shopping carts when mom turns her head.

Another nontraditional type of qualitative research is the immersion experience. There's no better way to gain an in-depth understanding of consumers than by becoming totally immersed in their culture and lives, even for a short period of time. We've sponsored several teen immersion experiences, titled "Wise Up to Teens!" in which for the better part of a day we immerse some of the country's top teen marketers in teenage life. We expose them to everything from the latest in popular culture to introspective teen-produced videos of teen life, to an opportunity to interact with and question teen Influencers.

We are experimenting with a new type of qualitative method: on-line research. A benefit of on-line teen research is that it can bypass the natural shyness and peer pressure that exists with in-person teen research. Teens who are quiet in focus groups can open up and offer information and insights in cyberspace.

On-line research has inherent problems, however. Unless you furnish teens with computers and modems or conduct the research in equipped schools, your on-line research will be limited to teens who are computer equipped. Teens with computers tend to be from more affluent households. Another problem with on-line research is that people often assume a different name and even a different personality when on-line. Because of this, it's important to recruit or at least screen respondents off-line. In this way, you will know the demographics, lifestyles, product or brand involvement, and other relevant characteristics of respondents before they come on-line. Another problem with on-line research is that you cannot see your respondents or adequately expose them to audio/visual stimuli. Because of this limitation, on-line research should not be looked at as a substitute for other qualitative research designs.

## The Stages of Qualitative Research: Recruitment

Qualitative research is done in five basic stages. The first stage, objective setting, has already been discussed. The second stage is recruiting teens for the study. Before recruiting, you need to consider sample composition, sample size, market selection (geography), recruiting method, and screening criteria.

**Sample Composition.** First, it's important to recognize that qualitative research does not provide quantitative results. The small size of the samples in qualitative studies precludes projecting the findings to any population. Still, you should choose qualitative participants carefully to ensure that the sample reflects your target market. If you have no specific teen target (and an objective of your research is to aid in targeting decisions), select a sample composed of different age, gender, ethnic, and geographic segments.

In focus groups, teens and children are most comfortable when they are with others of a similar age, gender, and background. Recruiting similar teens aids in the bonding of the participants, eliciting actionable answers. Consequently, you should conduct separate focus groups for boys and girls. Many teens do not feel comfortable with the opposite sex. If placed in a mixed-gender group, they feel inhibited and do not participate freely. Separating teens by gender will make your research more focused and productive.

Whenever possible, recruit by grade rather than age because grade is a better discriminator of lifestyle. A 14-year-old might be in junior high, middle school, or high school. A 14-year-old in high school will bring different experiences to a group than a 14-year-old in eighth grade. Similarly, when recruiting older teens, an 18-year-old could be in high school, college, or out of school and in the work force. Strive to keep the grade range in focus groups narrow, including no more than one or two grades in a single focus group such as seventh and eighth graders or eleventh and twelfth graders. If you must recruit by age rather than grade, keep the age range narrow, spanning no more than two single years.

To economize on the number of focus groups for a project, consider eliminating the middle grade group. If your target is 13-to-17-year-olds (or approximately eighth to twelfth grade), for example, conduct focus groups with eighth and ninth graders (in middle school) and eleventh and twelfth graders, eliminating tenth graders.

As is true with adult research, do not recruit respondents (except for panel research) who are recent research participants. The responses of experienced participants may be conditioned by their previous experience, particularly among teens.

**Sample Size.** Generally, a few focus groups are enough to achieve the objectives of most qualitative research projects. In general, conducting two to four focus groups of one gender/age cell is sufficient. Any more than that and the responses become repetitive.

The size of each focus group will depend on your research objective and the gender of the participants. A large group of girls typically is more manageable than a large group of boys, who are more likely to become rowdy and lose focus. Typically, full focus groups are composed of eight to ten participants, although we try to dissuade our clients from seating more than seven or eight. You should always over-recruit by 25 percent to make up for last-minute cancellations, no-shows, or respondents who do not qualify during on-site prescreening. Always pay the extras whom you send home.

We prefer small groups (known as minigroups) of four to six respondents simply because they are more productive. Even if eight or ten show up for a focus group, we handpick the more desirable participants to keep the group as small as the client will allow. To increase the number of respondents in qualitative research, it's better to conduct more small focus groups rather than add respondents to your scheduled groups. Although fewer individuals take part, each person gets to say more, which is the main idea of qualitative research. A small group also makes it easier for rapport to develop between the moderator and the group, and among respondents. The downside of a small group is that a few particularly quiet or inarticulate participants can account for a third to half of the group. This makes screening for expressive respondents critically important.

With one-on-ones and pairs, you typically need only a relatively small number of interviews to obtain insights for next-step decision making. Generally, a sample of 15 to 25 interviews is sufficient. The number will vary depending on the specific project objectives and the number of gender/age segments you want to explore. Most of the time, patterns begin to emerge after the first five to seven interviews. The remaining interviews tend to confirm those patterns and allow the moderator to probe outlying or emerging issues.

**Market Selection (geography).** Depending on your project's objectives, try to conduct research in more than one market. This is important for assessing any regional differences and also for diversifying your respondents. This is particularly true if your objective is to gauge the appeal or personal relevance of an ad or product. Texas teens may find different things appealing or relevant than New York teens. But if the purpose of your research is to learn whether your ad communicates its message (rather than testing for relevance or appeal), then it is less important to include more than one market. Ads that communicate in Dallas should also communicate in Manhattan, unless they contain language or symbols that are regionally specific.

If budget constraints dictate that you can conduct only two or three focus groups, you can consider midwestern teens reflective of the American teen population as a whole. Of course, if your teen target is defined geographically, then your research must be conducted in those geographic markets.

**Recruiting Method.** There are several ways to recruit teenage respondents for qualitative research.

1. Focus-group facilities provide lists of teens from their database of prescreened respondents, segmented by demographics. The best facilities keep notes on respondents, such as the type of research in which the teen previously participated and whether the teen contributed fully in the research or was a behavior

problem. Be careful not to include teens who were behavior problems in a group setting in focus groups, but you can include them in one-on-one interviews. The rowdiest teens can make the most productive one-on-one respondents.

2. Specialized lists or samples of particular teen segments can be purchased from traditional list houses.

3. Teens can be recruited through random-digit dialing or through-the-phone book methodology (using telephone directories as a base from which to locate teen respondents).

When a sample is particularly tough to recruit, we often resort to guerrilla tactics, such as placing ads in school newspapers and posting signs where teens (or a particular teen segment) hang out, like clubs, parks, athletic fields/facilities and certain stores. These ads and signs should stress the fee for participating, and it should be significant (such as $50) to entice "low incidence" teens. Be careful: no-show rates are higher for recruits obtained by these methods than by telephone.

**Screening Criteria.** Every potential participant should meet certain criteria before you include them in your study. Not only must they be the right age and gender, but they must also meet project-specific criteria such as product category involvement or participation in a particular activity. In addition, it is crucial to adequately screen for articulation to ensure that participants can express themselves in a group or when discussing a sensitive topic with an outsider. The screening technique for articulation can be almost any open-ended question, such as, "What's the best book you've read lately and why?" or "What's the toughest thing about being a student in your school? Why do you say that?"

The teens who pass the articulation screen are those who do not hesitate to speak up. They express themselves clearly and intelligently. Their actual answers to these questions are less important than the manner in which they express themselves. At this stage in your project, you may be at the mercy of hired recruiters, especially if the type of teen you need for a study is difficult to find. Recruiters hate to drop people who qualify all the way through except for articulation. But always stand firm on this issue. Make sure recruiters do not invite inarticulate or overly quiet people, even if it means making another 100 phone calls to find the right people.

To find a good recruiter, we recommend the booklet titled *Impulse Survey of Focus Facilities*, which rates focus-group facilities across the country based on recruiting, the quality of the facility site, personnel, and so on. The ratings are a compilation of moderators' experiences with facilities, collected through an annual survey. The booklet is available from Impulse Research Corporation, 8829 National Blvd., Suite 1006, Culver City, CA 90232; telephone 310-559-6892; e-mail bnovick@netcom.com.

While we enjoy a luxurious focus-group facility as much as anyone, when selecting a facility there's one criterion that's first and foremost: the quality of its recruiting. We keep a detailed log of our experiences, positive and negative, with every facility we use, creating our own rating system that each moderator adds to after completing research. Because back rooms, rectangular tables, and ubiquitous bowls of M & M's make Des Moines seem like Tucson, you should keep your own notes on each facility so that you can refer to them later if you ever need to do more research in that market.

It's also important to work closely with focus-group facilities so that they clearly understand and properly adhere to the screening questionnaire, which sets out to ensure that each participant is fully qualified. The screener questionnaire probes five areas:

1.  Demographic, product usage, or other attributes specific to the study.

2.  Parents' occupations. As with adult research, you should avoid recruiting participants in households with members who are employed in advertising, marketing research, or in any other capacity within the research industry or in your business.

3.  Recent participation in other market research projects. We recommend not recruiting someone who has participated in a study in the past 12 months or in more than two studies in the past three years. Experienced respondents may be sensitive to the types of answers desired, producing biased results.

4.  Articulation. Avoid recruiting teens who cannot express themselves coherently in a controlled setting or who are at all reluctant to contribute to a discussion.

5.  Trendsetting. For many research projects, it may be most productive to recruit teens who are viewed as the "coolest," whose lead is followed by others. By asking "cool" teens about a product, service, or new concept, you gain insight into what teen opinion leaders think and feel. To put it bluntly, why waste time and money asking teens whose opinions don't matter to their peers to comment on new products or advertising? One way to find "cool" teens is to ask a research company to screen for them. At TRU, for example, our screen for Influencers is based on responses to about a dozen key measures in our syndicated study. We give focus-group facilities a list of these measures with a grid of possible responses so that they can determine who's eligible and who isn't, making "cool" a screening criterion.

Another way to screen for "cool" teens is to develop special "trendsetter" questions for the category you're researching. You should design these questions as statements with which respondents either agree or disagree (with "strongly" and "somewhat" subcategories). When developing a new videogame accessory, for example, you may want to talk to teens who are the earliest adopters in this category. You can help locate these trendsetters through agree/disagree statements such as: "My friends and other kids at school look to me as kind of an expert when it comes to videogames." Or, "When a new videogame comes out, I've got to be the first to get it!"

The third way to get trendsetters (if you have the budget to do so) is to over-recruit. If your plan is to seat 6, recruit 12. Then take the potential respondents into a room in groups of two or three and briefly question them in key areas. For example, ask: "What's the last thing you've done that's gotten you in trouble? Or "What's your worst habit?" Or, "Describe yourself!" It's easy to spot the trendsetters among respondents. Because the major criterion of "cool" is good looks, physical appearance alone will help you discriminate between respondents, especially combined with key discussion points. You should keep notes about whom to eliminate as the discussion proceeds, and ask the backroom observers to do the same. Then compare notes and make a decision. This process will end up costing you more for recruiting, but it will go a long way toward putting together a group of productive respondents.

Probably the most effective, and certainly the most expensive, technique for finding trendsetters is known as pyramidal recruiting. Because of its high cost (up to $600 per respondent for recruiting), most companies use this technique only when developing longitudinal panels, which amortizes the recruiting cost over several projects. To recruit in this way, you should go to the places teens hang out and ask the adults and teens there to recommend trendsetters. Then talk to the trendsetters and ask them to recommend trendsetters. Typically, they recommend others. Talk to those others and ask them to recommend trendsetters. If trendsetters recommend themselves, interview them intensively. You should deem only the most qualified as eligible to participate.

Levi Strauss & Co., for one, is committed to a pyramidal recruiting program. I've moderated several sessions using Levi's panel members, who were successfully recruited to be fashion trendsetters. Levi's research and product managers believe their money has been well spent on developing this panel. The company is able to have its ideas evaluated by teens who are not only discriminating about fashion themselves, but who are the first to adopt new fashions: they are the teens other teens closely follow.

Whether you're recruiting adults or teens for qualitative research, cash is almost always the best incentive, typically around $50. If the research is at a facility where there's a fee for parking, pay extra. If a parent will be driving, pay the parent a little extra, around $10. We usually rely on the local focus-group facility's recommendation on how much to pay, since they know their market best, although we believe in always erring on the high side. Saving a few dollars is short sighted compared to the risk of not filling a group or an interview slot.

It's also important to pay "floaters" more (about $10 to $20 more) than scheduled one-on-one or buddy pair participants because their time commitment is greater than a scheduled participant's. (Floaters are over-recruits, who substitute for no-shows.) We usually ask them to cover two or three interview sessions.

The exception to using cash as an incentive is when your company has a product to give away that is more valuable to participants than cash. The giveaway needs to be universal in appeal so that it attracts the needed teens. Examples of noncash incentives that work well are athletic shoes (get the respondent's size during the screening interview), videogames or accessories, and jeans (again, get the size).

Finally, talk to the teen's parents, asking permission to include their child in the research (remember, it's the parents who will be driving younger teens to the interview). If you will be asking teens to taste food or beverages, you should get the parents' written permission, specifically asking them whether their children are allergic to any foods. We never reveal a client's identity, but if the subject matter is sensitive, we explain to teens and parents the topic to be discussed. For example, when we did a project for the Partnership for a Drug-Free America on inhalants, we recruited only teens who felt comfortable talking to us about drugs and whose parents had no objection to our discussing the matter with their children.

When participants arrive at the research facility, it's important to re-screen them. The re-screen can reveal changes in a participant's age, product/category involvement, or other factors affecting their eligibility.

Most of the qualitative research we conduct is held at established focus-group facilities, complete with one-way mirrors, microphoned rooms, kitchen facilities, and so on. Typically, focus-group facilities handle recruiting in their local area. Sometimes we conduct focus groups outside facilities, including parks, respondents' homes, schools, stores, camps, restaurants, and community centers.

A one-way mirror offers the least obtrusive method of observing focus groups and other qualitative research. In rooms without one-way mirrors, you can set up a video camera with a monitor in another room with the observers.

An increasing number of companies are conducting research at venues that are less artificial than traditional focus-group facilities. If a more natural environment adds to the comfort level of respondents and enhances discussion, then nontraditional settings have real merit, as long as everyone feels comfortable and on equal terms. In-home research, for example, should be conducted only among family members or close friends, so that all participants feel equally comfortable in the home. A traditional focus-group facility is a great equalizer. If respondents are strangers to one another, the facility puts them on equal terms.

Friends of mine own and direct one of the country's top boys' summer camps, Camp Kawaga, located in Minocqua, Wisconsin. We conducted a recent project for them, interviewing parents of campers, parents of potential campers, and campers themselves. The findings were helpful in evaluating camp programs and in recruiting campers. We conducted the first two phases of the research by telephone. But when interviewing the boys themselves, there was no better place than at the camp, which allowed the boys to relax and talk candidly. It was especially rewarding to conduct "focus groups" during rest hour, when the boys were lying around on their bunks. There could be no more natural setting for them to really open up about camp than in the cabins they love and share.

## The Stages of Qualitative Research: Focus-Group Discussions

The third stage of qualitative research (after setting objectives and recruiting participants) is designing the discussion guide, including any projective exercises that might be used. The guide summarizes the areas to be covered during the discussion or interview, including the topics in the order that you plan to address them, the length of time to be spent on each topic, and the issues to be emphasized. The guide becomes a check to make sure each research objective will be fully addressed. It also aids the moderator/interviewer in covering all the important points. It guides the flow of the discussion and ensures that you don't dwell too long on any one topic.

The most effective topic guide resembles a brief outline, listing subjects and key phrases rather than complete sentences or questions. This structure allows the moderator flexibility in phrasing questions. Flexibility, in turn, allows the moderator to respond to unexpected responses or to probe topics that may surface during the discussion.

A guide typically begins with general questions about a research category, then moves on to specific areas of inquiry about your product, brand, or marketing idea. The initial broad discussion allows the moderator to uncover participants' general feelings about a category without biasing them toward a particular product or brand.

As with adult focus groups, the moderator of teen focus groups first explains the ground rules. We start by asking whether anyone has ever participated in a discussion group before. If someone has, we ask that person to explain what's expected. Most of the time, the respondent will use the word "opinion." If she or he doesn't use the word, we do. As we always do in our focus groups with children, we usually ask teens to quickly define "opinion," making sure that somebody says the words, "it's what you *think* or *feel*."

We also tell them about the one-way mirror (if we're in a focus-group facility), explaining that a couple of our friends are sitting behind the mirror and taking notes because "what you say is very important to us." By stressing the importance of their participation and their opinions, teens take the task more seriously, which results in a more focused discussion.

Some of our clients are reluctant to tell participants about the one-way mirror, convinced that this will inhibit teens. But if you don't tell teens about it, they will undoubtedly figure it out on their own (especially in a group). Either someone who has taken part in a group before tells everyone else about it at an inopportune moment, or someone sees movement behind the glass. Teens' sudden discovery of the one-way mirror interrupts the flow of the group and can cause them to lose trust in the process and the moderator. When you tell teens about the mirror in the beginning, it becomes a nonissue. Usually, they will wave at the mirror and forget about it a moment later.

We also explain to respondents that they are being taped (sometimes videotaped in addition to audio). After telling them they are being taped (again, because what they say is important), they quickly accept being recorded. We also tell them that, for us, the group is "kind of like school. We have to write a report, and we usually listen to the tape on the airplane." So we ask them to speak loudly and one at a time so that we'll be able to understand the tape later.

We reassure respondents that this is not school and that we're not teachers. They do not need to raise their hands, nor are there rules regarding appropriate language. This accomplishes two things: some teens have an easier time articulating their feelings if they can use slang or don't have to be concerned with how they express their feelings; and it changes the tone from authoritative to cooperative. After all, we want to hear real feelings, expressed using real language.

We never recruit more than one participant from a single school, except with buddy pairs. This reduces the likelihood that any two participants will know one another, since it's important for all participants to be on equal ground. Either everybody knows everybody (as in the case of the Camp Kawaga research), or everybody knows only one other participant (buddy pairs), or nobody knows anybody (most common).

Peer pressure operates in every teen community. Even in focus groups where nobody knows anybody else, there's peer pressure. We address this issue at the beginning of the group discussion. We ask the group (already knowing the answer), "Does anybody here know anybody else?" When everyone sees that the answer is "no," we say, "Well that means none of you will ever see anyone here again. So, there's no reason to care what anybody else thinks!" The teens typically react to this statement by quickly looking around the room, smiling slightly with relief.

This reassurance is an effective segue to our next ground rule (which really needs to be emphasized when working with teens): "We're not here to agree! So if you're the only one who disagrees or has a different opinion, that's great. As long as it's your honest opinion."

Following the explanation of the ground rules is the warmup, which aids in getting participants comfortable with speaking in front of the group and in bonding the group members. In addition to giving their first names, grade level, and school, we ask teens to share an experience or personal characteristic. One of our favorite warmups is: "What have your parents (teacher, boyfriend, girlfriend) recently done that has really pissed you off?"

Regardless of the response, it's important that the moderator verbally or nonverbally show support for each respondent. Usually, other participants will say, "Yeah, that's happened to me too," or "That would really piss me off, too!" Strangers can quickly grow close by hearing about their common experiences.

To elicit the most actionable and productive focus-group discussion, the moderator should follow five rules:

1. The tone of the group should be friendly, open, and fun. Each participant should feel comfortable and respected.

2. Participants should do most of the talking. The moderator's role is to stimulate and guide discussion, not to participate.

3. Teen hierarchy is so strong that even in a group of strangers, leaders will exert themselves. Moderators should not allow one person to dominate the discussion. Similarly, if one or two participants are hesitant to speak up, the moderator should call upon them periodically, asking them to contribute and reinforcing their productive comments.

4. Teens (fortunately!) do not always agree. It's important to hear differing opinions and avoid forcing a consensus. If it appears that some participants are following the crowd, the moderator should play devil's advocate to elicit honest responses.

5. We often ask participants to write down their opinions or ratings on a piece of paper to minimize peer pressure. After they commit their thoughts to paper, teens are more likely to be forthcoming about their feelings. There are a variety of specialized techniques you can use to elicit honest responses from teens. Some of those we use most often are discussed next.

**Teen Match.** We often engage teens in an exercise we call "Teen Match" at the beginning of a focus group. This technique is especially effective in evaluating new concepts or products. In the exercise, we ask teens to name the different teen groups in their school, such as jocks, nerds, headbangers, wannabes, preps, etc. The moderator writes down the names of the teen types on a chalkboard or easel pad, explaining that they will return to the list later for further discussion. Toward the end of the focus group (after full discussion and evaluation of the test product, service, or concept) the moderator returns to the list, asking the group to match the test product to the teen type to whom it would most appeal. Because affiliation and hierarchy are so important in teens' lives and can shade their opinions about any new idea, this exercise allows you to get a uniquely teen perspective on the status, image, and potential success of the product among teens.

**Card Sorting for New Concepts and Positionings.** When testing new concepts, we often use a card-sorting technique. Card sorting offers a visual as well as physical way to keep young respondents focused. First, the moderator shows the group a series of concepts or positionings on a large board. The concepts should be as complete as possible yet simple, because younger teens in particular have difficulty conceptualizing. Each concept should be as distinct as possible to help respondents to discriminate among them. Each should offer a visual reference, concept name, headline, description, and consumer benefits. After the group has viewed the list of concepts, the moderator hands a stack of cards to each participant, each card describing one of the concepts. The moderator asks the participants to split the deck into two piles, one for the concepts they like and one for the concepts they don't like. Finally, the moderator asks them to stack the cards in each pile in order of likability. This exercise provides an effective springboard for discussing each concept in depth. Depending on the number of concepts tested, one or two usually fall out of favor and another few rise to the top. Then a discussion on how to improve, modify and combine the best ideas can begin.

**Product/Brand Sorts.** Similar to concept sorts, this technique requires respondents to sort live products and brands. A product sort can reveal teens' unique perspectives: how they categorize products; what they believe to be the competitive set; and how they compare products on a wide range of attributes from "cool" and "fun" to size, shape, taste, and function.

**Personification.** To best understand brand imagery among teens, we often give respondents pictures of a variety of unfamiliar people. We ask participants to choose the picture of the person who would use each of the tested brands.

**Symbol Boards.** In addition to exposing teens to pictures of unfamiliar people, we show them pictures of celebrities, animals, settings, athletic-shoe or apparel brands, cars, and so on, asking them to project their feelings onto the pictures. We say, for example, "If [the tested] brand were an animal, what kind of animal would it be?" The insight is in the reasons respondents choose a particular symbol to represent a brand. The actual choice is less important. A respondent who chose a basset hound to represent a brand could explain her choice by saying the basset hound is "cool" or she could say it is "stupid." Either way, the answer is revealing.

**Word Lists.** In this exercise, we give respondents lists of words and phrases and ask them to circle those that best describe the brand in question. Actually giving teens words is the key to doing this successfully. If you simply ask teens to offer up words without a list, respondents have much greater difficulty and the process is far less productive. By carefully choosing the words on the list and offering enough choices, the results should provide a clear picture of how teens feel about a particular brand.

**Wish Lists.** To provide insight into new product development or to enhance existing products or concepts, we often ask respondents to express their opinions with "wishes." The rules of the wish list are simple: there are none. When teens are told that anything goes, their natural creativity is engaged to produce new product ideas, modifications, and enhancements.

**Individual and Team Tasks.** Because teens are so affected by peer pressure, even in focus groups, we often assign each participant a task and then ask him or her to present the results of the assignment to the group. In this way, respondents who are reluctant to speak up when sitting around a table are forced to contribute. More often than not, these reticent participants offer valuable insights. In a similar way, pairing teens and forcing them to work with someone they don't know can produce insights that might not emerge through group discussion.

**Role Playing.** Teens (and even children) can effectively participate in role-playing exercises. If an objective of your research is to understand the roles teens play vis-a-vis significant others (parents, siblings, friends, teachers, grandparents, store clerks, celebrity endorsers, etc.), asking participants to take on the significant other role can provide great insight into the interpersonal dynamics of teenagers and the adults around them.

**Ideation Sessions.** If handled properly, teens can brainstorm effectively. "Teen Tank" sessions are focus groups specifically designed to generate ideas for new products, services, promotions, advertising ideas, or names for products. These sessions include participants who are screened not only for articulation, but also for creativity. During these groups, teens work through a series of ideation exercises and excursions in which they examine current attitudes and behaviors, identify current needs and solutions, create wish lists for new ideas or solutions, and design a product or service. Many of the exercises in these sessions involve role playing, where teens take on the role of the product, a manufacturer, a current user, or a competitor. Other exercises include word associations, storytelling, or clay creations. Brainstorming sessions are usually more productive when composed of older teens, who are cognitively more advanced and able to be more productive for a longer period of time.

## The Stages of Qualitative Research: One-on-One, Buddy Pair, and Parent-Teen Pair Interviews

Warmups for these interviews are just as important as in focus groups. Though a respondent doesn't need to get comfortable with a group, it is important for the moderator to establish rapport with the teen. Often the warmup conversation centers around a teen's recent experience with his or her parents or friends.

During the warmup, the moderator establishes the tone of the interview. It is important for respondents to feel they are in a friendly, comfortable environment and can talk openly. If the subject matter is delicate, the respondent must feel that the moderator will not pass judgment.

Buddy-pair interviews (two friends who have been recruited together but independently meet a project's screening criteria) can be highly productive. Having a friend next to them increases teens' comfort level and encourages dialogue. Good friends are also comfortable in disagreeing with each another. In fact, at the start of a buddy-pair interview, we ask the two friends if they always agree with each other. Of course, they say no. We use this response to emphasize the need for independent thinking and encourage open disagreement. Still, if an objective of the research is to evaluate communication, we always have each respondent commit his or her responses to paper before the discussion, to minimize any bias.

A parent-teen interview is especially helpful in exploring how teens request, influence, or actually purchase a product or classification of products. We usually begin these sessions by warming up with both parties together, then we talk separately to the teen to get his or her perspective on the teen-parent dynamic. We excuse the teen and have a similar discussion with the parent. Then, we bring the teen back in, and, with the parent in the room, discuss and come to an understanding of any contradictions between their perspectives. The most insightful findings often come from discussing the conflicts.

## The Stages of Qualitative Research: Debriefing

Debriefing is an important step in a qualitative study. During debriefing, the moderator and all personnel who have observed the focus groups or interviews review the session, focusing on key findings and observations. During this review, you should determine whether all your research objectives were satisfactorily addressed and itemize the relevant insights.

Debriefing is also helpful in providing direction to decisionmakers who have viewed only one session or a few of the groups.

The debriefing session is an excellent time to discuss the strengths and weaknesses of stimuli used in the groups. For example, the debriefing discussion may result in the elimination or revision of some less-than-positively received concepts or positionings, confusing storyboards, etc. Moreover, it is an opportunity for both the client and the moderator to review the key findings and decide on the next steps for the remaining groups/interviews. One of the benefits of qualitative research is the ability to quickly change direction, therefore debriefing (formal or informal) should focus on any necessary changes for the remaining interview sessions.

Because it is difficult to take detailed notes of what every respondent said during a focus group, the debriefing is an ideal time to review what teens said as well as what they meant. This helps avoid misinterpreting respondents' intentions. We are also careful during the debrief not to internalize any client or agency bias.

## The Stages of Qualitative Research: Reporting

The fifth and final stage of qualitative research is the report. When your interviewing is complete, your project is not. It's rare that everyone who will be involved in the findings actually is present during the research. For some, the only way to find out about the research in-depth is to read the report. And for all, the report serves as a document that summarizes the findings, notes implications, and lays out recommendations. On occasion, the report will serve only as a file filler because decisions have been made during research and finalized during debriefing. In these cases, a report is not as important but is still necessary. As your company's personnel changes and issues are revisited, the report may be the company's only link to the research findings.

There are alternatives to a comprehensive written report. First, for key management unable to attend the research, we often give a next-day telephone debrief. Although this is less formal and less comprehensive than an in-person presentation, it's more timely and often more actionable.

A second alternative is a one- or two-page topline report that includes key insights, conclusions, and recommendations. Details and verbatim responses that expand upon, add flavor to, support, or document the topline can come later. From a business point of view, clients appreciate the quick topline, because it often saves them from writing and issuing a summary themselves.

Regardless of the reporting method, it's always worthwhile to stage a formal presentation of the findings. This gives everyone (including those who were not present at the research) the opportunity to learn the results, discuss implications, and decide on next steps.

## Quantitative Research Among Teens

Quantitative research among teens is similar to that among adults. But because of the cognitive and developmental differences between teens (especially young ones) and adults, quantitative research needs to be designed with this in mind. Here is a brief overview of the basic quantitative methods: mail surveys, telephone interviews, and mall-intercept studies and their relative advantages and disadvantages in researching teens.

### Teen Mail Surveys

**Sample.** Can be a large, nationally representative sample, although there is less control over the final sample size and composition than with phone or mall-intercept studies. Samples can be purchased from a survey research company.

**Responsiveness.** Teens receive few pieces of mail, so they tend to be more responsive than adults. Cash incentives and follow-up phone calls increase response rates.

**Stimuli.** Mail allows teens to be exposed to visual stimuli, such as pictures of packages, logos, characters, etc.

**Age Appropriateness.** We do not recommend mail surveys for those under the age of 12.

**Cost.** Relatively inexpensive on a cost-per-interview basis, because long questionnaires can be sent to large numbers of people.

**Timing.** Longer turnaround time than other quantitative methods. Average project length is about eight weeks.

## Teen Telephone Surveys

**Sample.** Can be a large, nationally representative sample recruited through random-digit dialing or from a purchased sample. As with qualitative research, telephone surveys allow you to eliminate respondents who have participated in research in the past 12 months, unless they are part of a panel. Also, respondents should not live in a household with members who are employed in advertising, market research, or in the client's industry.

**Responsiveness.** Generally, teens are willing participants, more cooperative than adults. Still, they have busy schedules, so fieldwork needs to be scheduled accordingly.

**Stimuli.** Telephone surveys do not allow you to expose teens to visual stimuli. Brief concepts, however, can be read to them.

**Age Appropriateness.** Appropriate for teens, but not for children under the age of eight. The telephone interviewers must be trained to work with teens and never sound condescending.

**Cost.** Generally less expensive than mall-intercept interviews, depending upon sample size.

**Timing.** Quick turnaround

## Teen Mall-Intercept Surveys

**Sample.** Since mall surveys are conducted only in selected markets, the sample will not be representative of the population as a whole. Still, this method can be an ideal way to set quotas in specific markets. You can recruit respondents at the mall, screen them, and invite them to an in-mall facility to complete the interview. Or, if the questionnaire is brief, you can conduct the interview at the point of interception. You can also pre-recruit respondents, which is particularly important for low-incidence segments (such as teen boys who do the major food shopping for their household and who buy a certain brand of snack chips). Pre-recruiting is more expensive, but it gives you more control over the final sample.

**Responsiveness.** Participation tends to be high, since malls are a favorite teen venue. Many teens think intercepts are fun.

**Stimuli.** This quantitative method is the best for exposing teens to visual stimuli, from concept boards to videotapes to food.

**Age Appropriateness.** Appropriate for teens, and especially appropriate for younger children because of the extra control of a face-to-face interview.

**Cost.** Tends to be the most expensive of the three quantitative designs on a cost-per-interview basis.

**Timing.** Depending upon mall traffic and incidence of teen shoppers, this can offer a relatively quick turnaround.

Once you have established the research objective and determined the data-collection method, the next step is to draft a questionnaire specifically designed for teens. If any multivariate analyses will be performed, design the questionnaire with this in mind.

Quantitative questionnaires for teens are similar in design and content to questionnaires for adults, but the questions must be worded in a way that is readily understood by teens and is not condescending. The questions should be more conversational in tone than those used for adults. They should not be overly inquisitive or too scientific-sounding. Most important, the questions should be fun to answer.

Teens usually do not have difficulty responding to open-ended questions. When probing, however, many prompts of "what else/anything else" may overly pressure teens to respond. Usually, one follow-up prompt of "what else" and one "anything else" will suffice, yielding pertinent information and avoiding created responses.

Teens are experienced in working with scaled questions, such as attribute ratings, because of their school experience. These types of questions are most productive if you limit the list to seven to ten attributes. When asking teens scaled questions, you should show the scale to respondents for quick reference. Cards work best in mall-intercept interviews. In telephone interviews, interviewers should ask respondents to jot down the scale. Make the scale as friendly as possible. Don't bore teens with dull scale descriptors.

You should pre-test the questionnaire among the youngest respondents to be included in the sample. If a questionnaire is understood by the youngest, it should be understood by the entire sample. In pre-testing, make sure teens understand the words on the questionnaire, what each question means, and any scales used. Verify the accuracy, logic, and flow of questions and skip patterns. If teens have difficulty with any of these elements, fix them and test again. Don't assume the fix works until it is checked once again with respondents!

In telephone or mall-intercept research, you must train interviewers to handle teenage respondents. They need to understand teen psychology and never assume a pedantic role. One way to get the right interviewers is to hire young adults who are not far out of their teen years themselves. Teens with attitude are often better handled by twentysomethings than by older adults.

# Conclusion

In making your case to corporate management as to why teens are a viable marketing target, you may face a daunting task. You must develop a rationale for investing considerable dollars in this fast-moving segment and persuade upper management that your company can succeed where others have failed. You must convince management that you can sell to teenage America.

Here are three key points to drive home:

**1. Teen spending is huge.** Teen purchasing power, combined with population trends, warrant aggressively pursuing this market.

Teen spending is on the rise, and few teens are saddled with payments that stifle adult spending, like rent, utilities, and groceries. Teens' considerable income is almost exclusively discretionary. They are consumers with a mission: they want to spend on whatever happens to please them. What a compelling advertising target!

Teens are adept enough at saving money to finance most big-ticket purchases; in fact, more than three-fourths have a savings account. So almost all products are well within a teen's reach. This includes everything from a favorite soft drink to the latest computer software.

And even when teens are not buying products themselves, they influence—both passively and aggressively—their parents' buying. Not only do their mothers know what cereal brands to buy for them, parents also seek their teenage children's counsel when buying a family computer or shopping for a stereo or VCR. (And, of course, all this buying and requesting shape their future attitudes about your brand.)

Perhaps the most exciting news about the teen market is that the teen population boom is just beginning. After 17 years of decline, which ended in 1992, the teenage population is expected to grow each year until the year 2010, at which time there will be more teens than ever before in the U.S. population.

**2. Teens can be reached.** There are more media vehicles with which to reach teens today than at any time in the past. Although teens' media schedule and preferences differ from those of adults and children, teens have a huge appetite for media. From teen magazines to alternative 'zines, from MTV to Fox to Channel One, and from place-based media and special events to local radio, media companies are rapidly developing more effective and cost-efficient ways to reach the nation's teenagers. Management's argument that the teen market is too elusive no longer holds water.

**3. Teens can be influenced by advertising and marketing.** We often tell gun-shy potential teen marketers that trying to understand and appeal to teens need not be so trying. Teens are not so enigmatic, so difficult to understand, and so fickle in their likes and dislikes, that they cannot be swayed by well-crafted advertising and marketing efforts.

In the past five to ten years, the collective knowledge about teens and an understanding of how to reach them has grown enormously, allowing more companies to create relevant and compelling marketing communications directed at teens. In fact, many of today's most successful brands are thriving in large part because of their teen efforts.

Go ahead, make the case to management. Tell them why and how the teen market can grow your business. By marketing to teens smartly and creatively, the reward will be well worth the risk.

# Index